CANADIAN GRAMMAR SPECTRUM

REFERENCE AND PRACTICE

George Yule

OXFORD
UNIVERSITY PRESS

OXFORD
UNIVERSITY PRESS

Oxford University Press is a department of the University of Oxford.

It furthers the University's objective of excellence in research, scholarship, and education by publishing worldwide. Oxford is a registered trade mark of Oxford University Press in the UK and in certain other countries.

Published in Canada by
Oxford University Press
8 Sampson Mews, Suite 204,
Don Mills, Ontario M3C 0H5 Canada

www.oupcanada.com

First Edition published in 2013

Oxford Practice Grammar: Intermediate was originally published in 2006. This edition is published by arrangement with Oxford University Press, Great Clarendon Street, Oxford OX2 6DP, United Kingdom.

Library and Archives Canada Cataloguing in Publication
Yule, George, 1947–
Canadian grammar spectrum 8 : reference and practice / George Yule.

Includes index.
Previously published as part of: Yule, George. Oxford practice grammar. Advanced, 2006.
ISBN 978-0-19-544837-5

1. English language—Grammar—Problems, exercises, etc.
2. English language—Textbooks for second language learners. I. Title.

PE1128.Y942 2012   428.2'4   C2011-903946-X

Printed and bound in Canada.

3   4   5   —   18   17   16

Credits

5   Excerpt from *Oxford Guide to British and American Culture* published by Oxford University Press © Oxford University Press, 1999.

33   Excerpt from "Homage to Switzerland," from the Short Stories of Ernest Hemingway. Scribner (Simon & Schuster Adult publishing group) © renewed 1961 by Mary Hemingway

55   Excerpted from *The English Patient* by Michael Ondaatje. Copyright © 1992 Michael Ondaatje. Reprinted by permission of McClelland & Stewart. Reprinted by permission of Bloomsbury Publishing Plc

71   Excerpt from *You Just Don't Understand* © 1990 Deborah Tannen

Illustrations: by Donna Guilfoyle/ArtPlus Ltd., except page 28 by Adrian Barclay.

Contents

Pronouns, substitution, and ellipsis

Adjectives and adverbs

Prepositions

Infinitives and gerunds

Reporting

Noun clauses

Relative clauses

Conditionals

Adverbial clauses

Connectors and focus structures

Review test

Appendix: Regular and irregular verbs

Glossary

Answer key

Index

Introduction

Canadian Grammar Spectrum is a series of books, each written at the appropriate level for you at each stage in your study of English. The series is intended for your use either in a classroom or when working independently on your own time.

The books are divided into two- to four-page units, each of which covers an important grammar topic. Each unit starts with an explanation of the grammar and this is followed by a set of practice exercises. A test at the end of each book gives the opportunity for more practice and enables you to assess how much you have learned. Answers to the exercises and the test are provided at the back of the book.

You may want to choose the order in which you study the grammar topics, perhaps going first to those giving you problems. (Topics are listed in the Contents page at the front of each book and in the Index at the back.) Alternatively, you may choose to start at the beginning of each book and work through to the end.

The emphasis throughout this book is on the meaning and use of the grammatical forms. The explanations of grammar are descriptions of how English works; they are a guide to help you understand, not rules to be memorized. It is often more effective to look at examples of English rather than to read statements about it, and the grammar explanations are supported by lots of examples of everyday conversational English.

Key to symbols

The symbol / (oblique stroke) between two words means that either word is possible. *I may/might go* means that *I may go* and *I might go* are both possible. In exercise questions this symbol is also used to separate words or phrases which are possible answers.

Parentheses ( ) around a word or phrase in the middle of a sentence mean that it can be left out. *There's (some) milk in the fridge* means that there are two possible sentences: *There's some milk in the fridge* and *There's milk in the fridge*.

The symbol ~ means that there is a change of speaker. In the example *How are you? ~ I'm fine, thanks*, the question and answer are spoken by different people.

The symbol ▶ in an exercise indicates that a sample answer is given.

Linking verbs

Linking verbs and complements

Linking verbs, such as **be** or **seem**, are followed by a complement that describes or identifies the subject of the sentence. Complements can be adjectives (1), noun phrases (2), or prepositional phrases (3).

1 *His parents **were Brazilian**.* • *That **isn't funny**!* • *It doesn't **seem possible**.* • *You **sound unhappy**.*
2 *I **am a student**.* • *Anna **became my best friend**.* • *Despite the scandal, he **remained prime minister**.*
3 *She said she **was on a diet**.* • *He **seemed in a good mood**.* • *Sometimes I **feel like an idiot**.*

We can use **seem** and **appear** as linking verbs with an infinitive and a complement (4). We can also use **seem** with or without **to be** before complements (5). **Seem** is less formal than **appear**.

4 *Bill **seems** to have no friends.* • *There **appears** to be a problem.* (NOT *There appears a problem.*)
5 *The man **seemed** (to be) lost.* • *Equal pay for everyone **seems** (to be) the best solution.*

We can use verbs describing our sense experiences (**feel, smell, taste**) or our opinions (**look, sound**) as linking verbs with adjectives (6) or with **like** before noun phrases (7).

6 *I **feel** great!* • *You **look** much better.* • *The food didn't **smell** good and it **tasted** terrible.*
7 *Her suggestion **sounded like** a good idea.* • *Your drawing **looks like** a cat.* (NOT *Your drawing looks a cat.*)

With some verbs (**make, find, call**) we can use adjectives and noun phrases as complements after the objects to describe or add information about the objects.

8 *That **makes** me angry.* • *They **found** the exam difficult.* • *She **called** him a fool.*
Note the word order: *Let's paint the wall white.* (NOT *Let's paint white the wall.*)

Linking verbs used to express change

We use **become** and **get** as linking verbs to discuss the result of change.

9 *The world is **becoming/getting** more crowded.* • *Everything will **get** worse before it **gets** better.*

We can use **become** (not **get**) as a linking verb with noun complements (10) and **get** (not **become**) in many common phrases describing actions (11). **Get** is less formal than **become**.

10 *Traffic jams **have become** a problem.* • *We **became** friends.* (NOT *We became to be friends.*)
11 *They won't **get** married.* • *He **got** dressed quickly.* • *Let's **get** ready.* (NOT *Let's become ready.*)

We can use **go** and **turn** to discuss change (12). We use **turn into** before a noun phrase for a complete change of state (13).

12 *I'll **go** crazy if I have to wait.* • *Our dog **is going** blind.* • *She **turned** pale.* • *The light **turned** green.*
13 *Joe **turned into** a maniac.* • *The caterpillar **turned into** a butterfly.* (NOT *The caterpillar turned a butterfly.*)

We use **come** and **grow** as linking verbs with adjectives in phrases that usually express slower change, unless modified by adverbs such as **suddenly** or **unexpectedly** (14). We can use **come** and **grow** before infinitives to describe gradual change (15).

14 *Dreams **come** true.* • *People **grow** old.* • *The days **grew** warmer.* • *The knot suddenly **came** loose.*
15 *As we **came to know** her better, we **grew to like** her a lot. We **came to see** things as she did.*

We use some verbs (**keep, remain, stay**) as linking verbs to talk about a situation not changing.

16 *Please **keep** quiet.* • *She **kept** busy.* • *Everything **remained** the same.* • *We tried to **stay** warm.*
Note that these verbs are not used with **to be**. (NOT *I'll keep to be quiet. We stayed to be awake.*)

A Choose an answer (a–f) for each question (1–6) and add the linking verbs below. Use the appropriate form of each verb.

appear, be, feel, look, sound, taste

1 What .... he like? (..)
2 Whom does she .... like? (..)
3 How does it .... ? (..)
4 Did he .... to be happy? (..)
5 How did he .... ? (..)
6 Does it .... fishy? (..)

a Angry and impatient.
b I'm sure he was smiling.
c No, it's more like chicken.
d He's kind and generous.
e Soft and comfortable.
f The actress Sarah Polley.

B Complete each paragraph with appropriate forms of the verbs from one group.

appear / be / look / turn   ~~seem~~ / smell / taste / ~~think~~
become / get / make / seem   feel / get / stay / turn

The writer of the guide book (▶) _seemed to think_ that the Maharani restaurant had the best Indian food. In her description, she wrote, "All the dishes were full of fragrance and flavour." In other words, she thought the food (1) .... wonderful and (2) .... delicious.

In her late teens, Janna fell in love with Ernesto and wanted to (3) .... married, but that topic always (4) .... him uncomfortable. To her intense disappointment, he later decided to (5) .... a priest.

Elena was reading a novel with a red dragon on the cover. It (6) .... like a large lizard with wings. The novel was a horror story, she said, full of people who (7) .... living normal lives but were actually vampires, and one character who (8) .... into a werewolf during the night of a full moon.

I didn't want the bananas to (9) .... too ripe and then (10) .... soft or squishy when I wanted to eat them, so I put them in the fridge. I was just hoping that they would (11) .... firm, but I didn't realize that the skins would (12) .... black.

C Correct the mistakes in the use of linking verbs in this text.

One Saturday afternoon when my younger sister Mona and I were teenagers, I was ~~becoming~~ _getting_ ready to go to a party. Mona hadn't been invited. It appeared a big problem for her. She went to be crazy because of it. She found some hair dye and she just decided to make blonde her hair, but she didn't do it right and her hair turned into bright orange. It also became orange her face, so she looked like really strange. When my mother saw her, she said Mona looked an orange balloon. After that, Mona got to be very upset and she started screaming with her hands over her ears. I just kept to be quiet during all that. My mother eventually calmed her down and we got some darker hair dye to make it look like better.

Compound and complex sentences

A **Write the numbers of appropriate examples in the spaces.**

Compound sentences

A compound sentence has two ☐ or more ☐ clauses joined by coordinating conjunctions: **and, but**, or **or**.

1 *You can take the bus **or** stay here **and** I'll drive you tomorrow, **but** I'm not driving tonight.*
2 *Dave slept **and** I read.* • *It wasn't cold, **but** I was shivering.* • *You must help us **or** we will fail.*

We usually leave out the same subject ☐, the same subject + verb ☐, or the same subject + auxiliary ☐ from later clauses in a compound sentence.

3 *They played well, but ___ lost. (They played well, but they lost.)* • *Martin smiled, ___ shrugged his shoulders, and ___ said nothing. (Martin smiled, he shrugged his shoulders, and he said nothing.)*
4 *She will come and ___ get those later.* • *You can take it or ___ leave it.* • *I am waiting and ___ hoping.*
5 *They have a cat or ___ a dog.* • *I like swimming, ___ football, and ___ watching TV.*
Leaving out the subject or other parts of the sentence is called ellipsis.

We usually leave out the same verb + object after an auxiliary verb in later clauses ☐, but the meaning is clearer when we leave out repeated objects or prepositional phrases from the first clause ☐.

6 *I'll wash ___ and peel the potatoes.* • *The Vargases have lived ___ and died in Managua for centuries.*
7 *I wasn't making a noise and the others were ___.* • *They may forget you, but I never will ___.*

We can emphasize the relationship between two clauses in compound sentences by using different combinations of conjunctions. They can express an addition ☐, an alternative ☐, a combination ☐, or a combination of negatives ☐.

8 *They **not only** clean houses, **but also** do repairs, painting, and other odd jobs.*
9 *You can **both** turn the TV on **and** change channels with the remote control.*
10 *I will **neither** sleep **nor** rest until this is over.* • *He **neither** speaks English **nor** understands it.*
11 *You can **either** go with us **or** stay here alone.* • *They must **either** pay you **or** give you time off.*

Complex sentences

We create complex sentences by joining two or more clauses with subordinating conjunctions such as **because, before, that**, and **which**.

12 *I couldn't sleep **because** I was thinking about all the work **that** I had to do **before** I could leave.*
Note that the same subject is repeated. (NOT ~~I couldn't sleep because was thinking.~~)
Others include **although, as, if, in order that, since, when, who**

Complex sentences contain relative clauses ☐, noun clauses ☐, and adverbial clauses ☐. We can put adverbial clauses, followed by a comma, at the beginning of complex sentences ☐.

13 *I didn't realize **that Brian wasn't feeling well**.* • *Did you know **that he was married**?*
14 *She liked the women **with whom she worked**, but she hated the dirty jobs **that they had to do**.*
15 *I had a shower **after I ran**.* • *He's still working **although he's 72**.* • *We won't play **if it rains**.*
16 ***If it rains**, the ground will be too muddy.* • ***Although he's 72**, he still walks to work every day.*

Compound-complex sentences

We form compound-complex sentences with three or more clauses joined by both coordinating and subordinating conjunctions.

17 *We hit a telephone pole **and** it shattered the glass on the front door **before** I managed to bring the bus to a halt.*
18 *Saj said, "I was so relieved **that** no one else was hurt, **but** I hoped the driver would survive."*

B Choose an ending (a–d) for each beginning (1–4) and add *and*, *but*, or *or*.

1 You can leave now (…)
2 He says he needs a knife (…)
3 She not only speaks Arabic, (…)
4 Sotiris usually washes the dishes (…)

a ……….. she can also read ……….. write it.
b ……….. dries them right away.
c ……….. stay ……….. help us finish the job.
d ……….. scissors to open the package.

C Fill in each blank with a verb or subject + verb from below.

came, got, had, seemed, stopped, talked, she came, he got, we had, it seemed, it stopped, we talked

1 Police allowed protests outside the meeting, but ………………… people trying to get inside.
2 When ………………… about religion or politics, ………………… very excited.
3 After ………………… home from her trip, we sat and ………………… for hours.
4 ………………… easier in the past because people just met, ………………… married, and
………………… kids.
5 If she got up early enough and ………………… downstairs, ………………… breakfast together.
6 The dog ran over to the door where ………………… and ………………… to be waiting for us
to go outside.

D Complete the definitions with these nouns and conjunctions.

~~heartache~~	heartbeat	heartburn		and (×2)	because	that	who
heart attack	heartbreak	heartthrob		as	or (×2)	which	whom

(▶) A …heartache…… is a feeling of great sorrow, anxiety ……or………… worry.

Your (1) ………………… is the action (2) ………………… sound of your heart
(3) ………………… it pumps blood through your body.
(4) ………………… is an intense feeling of sadness (5) ………………… something bad has
happened, such as the end of a relationship.
A (6) ………………… is a celebrity (7) ………………… is very attractive (8) …………………
with (9) ………………… people fall in love.
A (10) ………………… is a sudden illness in (11) ………………… the heart beats violently.
It causes great pain (12) ………………… sometimes death.
(13) ………………… is a burning sensation in the chest (14) ………………… is caused by
indigestion.

E Add these conjunctions and appropriate forms of the verbs to the description.

and, because, but, if, which, who, live, not like, see, tell

A neighbourhood watch is an arrangement by
(1) ………………… people (2) …………………
(3) ………………… in a particular area watch each
other's houses (4) ………………… (5) …………………
the police (6) ………………… they (7) …………………
anything suspicious. Many people have formed local
neighbourhood watch groups to try to prevent crime,
(8) ………………… others have refused to join them
(9) ………………… they (10) ………………… the idea
of being watched by their neighbours.

Present Perfect, Past Perfect, and Simple Past

Present Perfect or Simple Past?

We use the Present Perfect when we think a situation has not ended (1) and the Simple Past when we think the situation ended (2).

1 *I **have lived** in Moose Jaw for a year.* • *She **has known** him since school.* • ***Has** Jason **been** sick?*
2 *I **lived** in Moose Jaw for a year.* • *She **knew** him in school.* • ***Was** Jason sick?*

We use the Present Perfect with time expressions for a period up to now (**lately, so far**) (3). We use the Simple Past with time expressions for a period that ended earlier (**last night, yesterday**) (4).

3 ***Have** you **seen** any good movies lately?* • *So far the new teacher **hasn't given** us any homework.*
4 ***Did** you **see** that movie last night?* • *I **didn't do** the homework yesterday.*
(NOT ~~Have you seen that movie last night? I haven't done the homework yesterday.~~)

We use the Present Perfect when we are referring to actions up to the present which might happen again (5) and the Simple Past for actions which we don't think will happen again (6).

5 *He **has written** two bestsellers and we hope his next book will do well.* • *He's **been** on TV; he's famous!* • *He **has** often **had** health problems.*
6 *She **wrote** several books of poetry in the last years of her life.* • *She **was** a teacher in Zambia.* • *She **had** three children.*

In clauses beginning with **after, as soon as**, and **when**, we can use the Present Perfect for completed actions in the future (7) and the Simple Past for completed actions in the past (8).

7 *After / As soon as / When he **has made** his copies, I <u>will do</u> mine.* (= He hasn't made his copies yet. Neither have I.)
8 *As soon as he **made** his copies, I <u>did</u> mine.* (= He made his copies first, then I made mine.)

A **Complete each paragraph with one set of verbs, using the Present Perfect or Simple Past.**

eat / not come / tell   become / have / hear   know / meet / start

I (1) .... Narmatha Paneer since we both (2) .... our jobs on the same day about five years ago. She is one of the smartest people I (3) .... ever ....

(4) .... you .... the good news yet? Jenny and Akiel (5) .... just .... parents! Jenny (6) .... a baby girl last night.

The plumber (7) .... me this morning, "I'll be back to finish the work as soon as I (8) .... some lunch." But now it's after three o'clock and he still (9) .... back.

B **Complete the dialogue with these verbs in the Present Perfect or Simple Past.**

ask, be (×2), have, make, not call, not eat, not know, not seem, say, tell

It's Monday afternoon. Edwin is at home, calling Toni at the office where they both work.
Edwin: Hi Toni, it's me.
Toni : Well, hello! Where (1) .... you .... all day? The boss
        (2) .... me this morning where you (3) .... , but
        he (4) .... to be looking for you or anything.
Edwin: What (5) .... you .... ?
Toni : I (6) .... him that I (7) .... Are you okay?
Edwin: I'm sorry I (8) .... you this morning. I (9) ....
        the flu since Saturday. I (10) .... anything for two days and it
        (11) .... me feel really weak. But I'll probably be there tomorrow.

Past Perfect or Simple Past?

When we are describing actions in the past, with the Simple Past (**won**), and we want to refer to actions even further in the past, we use the Past Perfect (**had won**).

> 9 *Ashleigh McIvor* **won** *an Olympic gold medal in 2010. She* **had won** *other medals in the past, but this was her first Olympic medal.*

With the Simple Past (**arrived**) in a **when**-clause, we use the Past Perfect (**had started**) in the main clause for an earlier action (10) and the Simple Past (**started**) for a later action (11).

> 10 *When he arrived in the morning, we* **had started** *work.* (= We started work before he arrived)
>
> 11 *When he arrived in the morning, we* **started** *work.* (= We started work after he arrived)

Note that two verbs in the Simple Past can suggest a cause and effect: *When I* **called**, *he came.*

In conditionals, we use the Past Perfect for something that did not happen (12) and the Simple Past for something that might happen (13).

> 12 *If you* **had come**, *you could have stayed with us.* • *If I'd* **known**, *I certainly would have helped.*
>
> 13 *If you* **came**, *you could stay with us.* • *If I* **saw** *anyone doing that, I certainly would try to stop it.*

We usually use the Past Perfect, not the Simple Past, with some adverbs (**already, just, still**).

> 14 *An ambulance came quickly, but the crash victim* **had already died**. (NOT ~~The crash victim already died.~~)
>
> 15 *The books* **still hadn't arrived** *when I left.* (NOT ~~They still didn't arrive when I left.~~)
>
> 16 *The students* **had just opened** *their books when the fire alarm went off.*

C **Choose an ending (a–d) for each beginning (1–4) and add these verbs in the Past Perfect or Simple Past.**

come, give, need, not finish, say, talk, work

1 He .... the money last week, (...)	a that you .... about that already.
2 You .... during the meeting (...)	b so I .... it to him then.
3 When he .... back later, (...)	c if she .... harder.
4 Ashley could have done much better (...)	d they still .... writing their reports.

D **Complete the text with these verbs.**

was (×2), explained, didn't eat, have gone, had cooked, hadn't eaten, were, went, didn't lock, have heard, had reached, hadn't locked

One of the four-year-olds in the reading group suddenly said, "This is the silliest story I
(1) .... ever ....!" I (2) .... in the middle of reading
"Goldilocks and the Three Bears" to the group. We (3) .... just .... the part
in the story where Goldilocks goes into the bears' house and eats some of the food from bowls on the table.

"Where (4) .... the bears?" he asked.

"Maybe outside or playing in the woods," I suggested.

"And their house was wide open? They (5) .... even .... the door
before going out?"

"Well, in the old days, people (6) .... their doors."

"And their food was on the table, but they (7) .... it before they
(8) .... outside?"

"Maybe they (9) .... it because it (10) .... too hot."

"If you (11) .... that meal, you wouldn't (12) ....
out and left it, would you?"

"Probably not, but it's just a story," I (13) .... weakly.

The future

A Write the numbers of appropriate examples in the spaces.

Future: will and shall

There is no single form used as the future tense. We can use **will** plus the base form of a verb to give or ask for information about the future ▢ and to talk about possible future actions when we make promises, requests, or threats ▢. We usually use contracted forms after pronouns (**'ll**) or in negatives (**won't**) unless we are being formal or emphatic.

  1 *We'**ll help** you clean up.* • *I **won't tell** anyone.* • ***Will** you please **go**?* • *Stop or I'**ll call** the police.*
  2 *The potluck **will be** on a Friday.* • *The meeting **won't start** until 9:30.* • *When **will** you **leave**?*

We sometimes use **shall** with **I** or **we** to express determination, or in questions to make offers or suggestions.

  3 *We will forgive, but we **shall** never **forget**.* • ***Shall** I **make** some coffee?* • *Let's talk later, **shall** we?*

Future Progressive, Future Perfect, and Future Perfect Progressive

We can use **will** + **be** + present participle (the Future Progressive) to talk about future actions in progress at a particular time ▢ and as a way of expressing plans or intentions ▢.

  4 *I'**ll be sending** out my application tomorrow.* • ***Will** you **be using** the car later or can I have it?*
  5 *Next week at this time, you **will be lying** on the beach and we'll all still **be slaving** away here.*

We can use **will** + **have** + past participle (the Future Perfect) to say that something will be completed by a particular time ▢. We use **will** + **have been** + present participle (the Future Perfect Progressive) when we look ahead to a future time and imagine an action lasting from a point before that time up to that future time ▢.

  6 *On the 10th of this month, I'**ll have been living** here for exactly two years.*
  7 *By next summer I'**ll have finished** my degree.* • *It's 5:30. **Will** Jay **have left** work already?*

Will or be going to?

We use **will** for a prediction based on past experience or knowledge ▢, especially in predictive conditionals ▢, and **be going to** for a prediction based on what we feel or think now ▢. We can use **would** or **was/were going to** when we describe a past prediction about the future ▢.

  8 *Oh, no, I think I'**m going to be** sick.* • *We've just heard that Kim'**s going to have** a baby.*
  9 *If you eat too much ice cream, you'**ll be** sick.* • *We'**ll do** okay if the test isn't too difficult.*
  10 *As soon as the victorious Canadian team lands in Vancouver, thousands of fans **will start** celebrating.*
  11 *When I was a teenager, I thought I **was going to be** a rock star and I **would** never **have** to work.*

We use **be going to** for a decision already made ▢ and **will** for a decision made at that moment ▢.

  12 *Her parents have said they'**re going to pay** for her tuition.* • *I've decided I'**m going to get** a new phone.*
  13 *I need someone to take this to the post office. ~ I'**ll go**!* • *That's the phone ringing. ~ I'**ll get** it!*

Simple Present and Present Progressive for the future

We can use the Simple Present for future events in a schedule or timetable ▢. We also use the Simple Present for future actions in clauses after subordinating conjunctions ▢. We can use the Present Progressive to discuss a future action we have planned or arranged ▢.

  14 *I'**m seeing** the doctor on Friday.* • *We'**re playing** tomorrow.* (NOT ~~It's snowing tomorrow.~~)
  15 *It won't matter what he **says** later.* • *I'll see you when I **get** back.* (NOT ~~I'll see you when I will get back.~~)
  16 *The new course **starts** in January.* • *I think Raul's flight **arrives** tomorrow morning.*

B Choose an ending (a–d) for each beginning (1–4) and add *will*, *will be*, or *will have been*.

1 Next April 21st .... my parent's silver anniversary. (...)
2 I'm sure everyone .... want to get an early start. (...)
3 Mr. Plante .... teaching his last English classes during May. (...)
4 My life as a student .... over at the end of this semester. (...)

a By then, he .... working here for 40 years.
b That means they .... married for 25 years.
c Do you realize that I .... in school for 80 percent of my life?
d .... you .... ready to leave at about 6 a.m.?

C Complete the text with the most appropriate forms of the verbs, using *will*, *be going to*, or the Simple Present.

be, give, have, make, not start, not stop

I was standing at the bus stop reading my horoscope in the newspaper. It said, "You (1) .... good moments and bad moments today." I looked up and saw the bus coming. Then I realized it (2) .... because it was already full. "Oh, no," I thought. "If I (3) .... walking fast, I (4) .... late for my first class!" I had just started walking when a car pulled up beside me and one of my classmates leaned out. "Hey Jean, get in, we (5) .... you a lift." It's amazing how the bad moments (6) .... the good moments feel so much better.

D Correct the mistakes in these sentences.

▶ An imminent event is one that ~~happens~~ <u>will happen</u> soon.

1 Please stop making so much noise or I report you to the supervisor.

2 As I was about to leave his office, Abed said, "Let's get together for lunch sometime, will we?"

3 They came and asked for people to help immediately, so Yvette jumped up and said, "I do it!"

4 When he is released next week, Bruce Gagnon will spend almost five years in prison for a crime he didn't commit.

5 I'm going to work on the report at home last night, but I had left all my notes in the office.

6 It's probably too late to call Elena. Do you think she'll go to bed already?

7 I'm not certain, but I guess it's raining later this afternoon.

8 Forthcoming books are those that we think to be available soon.

9 I can't believe that you'll sit on a plane to Panama while I'm driving to work tomorrow morning.

10 If I'll finish before you, I wait for you outside.

11 Will Stefan to get these boxes later or is to take them now?

12 I must get to the post office before it'll close or the package doesn't arrive in time for Jodi's birthday.

Complex modals

We form the modal perfect with a modal before **have** plus a past participle.

1 *Nikhil **may have taken** your book. He **shouldn't have done** that.* (NOT ~~He shouldn't done that.~~) •
*Obviously, he **must have done** something earlier that brought him bad luck.*

We form the modal progressive with a modal before **be** plus a present participle.

2 *Alex **shouldn't be acting** so confident. He **should be studying**.* (NOT ~~He should studying.~~)

We form the modal perfect progressive with a modal before **have been** plus a present participle.

3 *I called, but she didn't answer. She **must have been sleeping**.* (NOT ~~She must been sleeping.~~)

We form modal passives with a modal before **be** (4) or **have been** (5) plus a past participle.

4 *Some things **cannot be explained** by reason.* • *This shirt **should be washed** by hand.*
5 *People **could have been injured** by falling icicles.* (NOT ~~People could have injured~~ ...)

A Complete these sentences with *be*, *have*, or *have been*.

▶ She shouldn't ...... *have* ...... taken Kerwood's dictionary. I'm sure he'll ...... *be* ......
looking for it later.

1 I was glad that my old computer could .... repaired. I would ....
hated to have to buy a new one.

2 Children may not .... left alone in the playground. They must ....
accompanied by an adult.

3 Where's Tony? He should .... helping you clean out the garage. I guess he must
.... forgotten about it.

4 We weren't tired. We could easily .... talked for another hour. But we would
probably .... asked to leave the restaurant. It was getting late.

B Write the eight completed sentences from Exercise A in the appropriate blanks below.

Prediction: **will, would, be going to, shall** ▶ ....*I'm sure he'll be looking for it later.*....

1 ....

Willingness, habits, and preferences: **will, would**

2 ....

Ability: **can, could, be able to**

3 ....

Permission: **can, could, may, might, be allowed to**

4 ....

Possibility: **may, might, can, could**

5 ....

Necessity: **must, have to, have got to, need to**

6 ....

Deduction: **must, have to, can't, couldn't**

7 ....

Obligation: **should, ought to, be supposed to, had better** ▶ *She shouldn't have taken Kerwood's dictionary.*

8 ....

C **Choose an ending (a–e) for each beginning (1–5) and add these forms.**

able to, will be, must be, ought, going to, can't, won't, must have, should be, may have been

1 You know there .... a test
  tomorrow (...)
2 Sarita isn't .... study
  at all (...)
3 I .... find my calculator (...)
4 We .... to check the
  timetable (...)
5 Marc's arm .... injured (...)

a so that we .... be late.
b so I .... left it somewhere.
c so she .... feeling very confident.
d so he probably isn't .... write.
e so you .... studying tonight.

D **Using a dictionary if necessary, complete the sentences with these adjectives and modals.**

advisable, inconceivable, regrettable, can't, should, will, hypothetical, inevitable, reluctant, might, shouldn't, wouldn't

1 Someone who says, "It is .... that the police didn't do something sooner" feels
  that the police .... have acted sooner.
2 If someone says it is .... to wait, it means that you .... act
  immediately.
3 When you describe something as ...., you are certain that it ....
  happen.
4 It was clear that he was .... to talk and we .... get any information
  from him.
5 If you say that something is ...., you mean that you .... imagine it
  at all.
6 When something is described as ...., it is based on an idea about what
  .... happen and not on a real situation.

E **Correct the mistakes in the use of modals in this text.**

A dilemma is a situation in which you have a choice and you are not sure what you should ~~to.~~ ^{do}

In my dilemma, I had a good job as an administrative assistant for a big company, but I really wanted

to become a teacher and I didn't could do that without going to university. If I decided to do that,

I knew I will have to quit my job and, as a student, I have much less money. I talked about my

dilemma with one of the other assistants and she warned me that I don't should give up such a

good job. She said that a young woman supposed to think about making as much money as possible,

not going to university. It really was a dilemma and I couldn't decided what I ought do. But then I

talked to my aunt Maria. She told me that she should go to university when she was younger. She

decided not to go and she regretted it. She thought that I should to give it a try. She said I didn't

should be afraid and that she may can help me pay for things with some money she had saved.

That was the end of my dilemma.

Modals of prediction, willingness, habits, and preference

Prediction: will, would, be going to, shall

We use **will** for predictions (1) and to indicate what we think is most likely (2).

1 *It **will** be cold tomorrow.* • *I **won't** finish this before Friday.* • *Who do you think **will** win?*
2 *The phone's ringing. That **will** be Kevin.* • *Don't call them now. They'll be sleeping.*

We use **will** for a predictable situation (3) and **would** for a hypothetical situation (4).

3 *He'll look better without that scruffy beard.* (= I think that he's going to shave it off.)
4 *He'd look better without that scruffy beard.* (= I don't think that he's going to shave it off.)

We use **will** plus the perfect for a prediction about an event that has already happened at some future time (5). We use **would** plus the perfect for a prediction about an imaginary past event or situation (6).

5 *Don't call at midnight. Everyone **will have gone** to bed.*
6 *Life in the Middle Ages was harsh and cruel. You **would have hated** it.*

We usually use **will** for predictions based on past experience or knowledge (7) and **be going to** for predictions based on what we feel or think now (8).

7 *There **will** be delays because of bad weather.* • *Too much coffee **will** give you a headache.*
8 *Oh, no, I think it's **going to** rain.* • *He's **going to** get a headache from drinking all that coffee.*

We use **be going to** for a decision already made (9) or when something is starting to happen (10).

9 *We're **going to** spend the weekend at home.* • *Chris and Nadia **are going to** get married in May.*
10 *Be careful—you're **going to** drop it!* • *Close your eyes. I'm **going to** give you a big surprise.*

We use **was/were going to** (not **would**) for past plans: *I **was going to** study law, but changed my mind.*

We use **shall** with I or we in questions when we make offers and suggestions or when we ask for suggestions (11). We can use **will** (or **shall**) to express determination (12).

11 ***Shall** I close the door?* • *Let's try again, **shall** we?* • *Where **shall** we go for lunch today?*
12 *I **will** (OR I'll) finish this if it kills me!* • *We lost a battle, but we **will** (OR we'll) never give up!*

A **Complete this dialogue with these forms.**

will, I'll, I'm going to, I'd, would, shall, you'll, I was going to, won't, would have

It's 7:30 a.m. on Thursday. Pam and Jim are awake, but still in bed. The phone rings.

Pam: Oh, that (1) .... be for me. Hello?

Mom: Hello dear. I was hoping it wasn't too early for you. I have to go downtown today and I was wondering if you (2) .... be able to meet me for lunch.

Pam: Oh, (3) .... love to, Mom, but (4) .... get my hair done at lunchtime. I (5) .... been free, but Janet called yesterday and changed my appointment from Friday to today. (6) .... get it cut on Friday so that it would be nice for Dad's birthday this weekend.

Mom: Ah, the birthday party! That's why I have to go downtown. (7) .... we just have a coffee later? When do you think (8) .... be finished at the hairdresser's?

Pam: Oh, she (9) .... be finished until 1:30 or 2:00. And then I have to get back to the office.

Mom: It's okay. I understand. (10) .... talk to you later.

Willingness: **will** and **would**

We use **will** to say we are definitely willing now (13) and **would** for willingness in the future or in conditional sentences (14). We also use **would** when we mean "willing, but not able to" (15).

13 *I **will** give you one more chance.* • *There are advisers here who **will** help and guide you.*

14 *Most people **would** pay more for better health care.* • *I **would** stay longer if they asked me to.*

15 *Can you help us carry these boxes? ~ Oh, I **would** help you, but I've injured my back.*

We use **won't** (= isn't willing to) or **wouldn't** (= wasn't willing to) to say that a person refuses to do something (16) and to describe things or machines as if they were people who are/were not willing (17).

16 *He's sick, but he **won't** go to the doctor's.* • *She had a lot of money, but she **wouldn't** lend us any.*

17 *The door isn't locked, but it **won't** open.* • *My car **wouldn't** start this morning.*

Habits and preferences: **will** and **would**

We can describe present habits or typical behaviour with **will** (18). We can use **would** for habitual actions in the past (19).

18 *Her children **will** break everything they touch.* • *Dino **will** just sit watching TV for hours.*

19 *I **would** try to swim across the lake every year.* • *Each summer we **would** visit my cousins.*
We say **used to** (not **would**) for past states: *I **used to** have a dog.* (NOT ~~I would have a dog.~~)

We use **would** (not **will**) with verbs expressing preferences (**like, love, prefer**) (20), especially in offers (21).

20 *I **would** prefer an early class.* • *I'**d** love to go on a cruise.* (NOT ~~I'll love to go on a cruise.~~)

21 ***Would** you like some tea or **would** you prefer coffee?* (NOT ~~Will you like some tea?~~)

We use **would** (not **will**) after the verb **wish** when we're talking about preferred actions.

22 *I wish she **wouldn't** smoke.* • *Don't you wish they **would** make it easier to recycle things?*
We don't use **would** to describe states: *I wish I had a car.* (NOT ~~I wish I would have a car.~~)

B **Complete each sentence with one pair of verbs and forms of *will* or *would*, where appropriate.**

be / hate, be / say, eat / need, give / go, have / like, play / stay, push / start

1 Even when she gets the flu, my friend Vivienne .... to see the doctor because she's afraid that he .... her an injection. She is terrified of needles.

2 We had an old car that .... on cold mornings unless we got out and .... it.

3 Ming: Carla wants to know if you .... a piece of chocolate cake.
   Bob: Tell her I .... normally .... two slices, but not while I'm on this strict diet.

4 When we were young, we .... always .... outside during the summer, but nowadays children .... just .... inside watching TV or playing video games all day.

5 I hope I .... never .... asked to work on a night shift because I .... having to go to sleep for most of the following day.

6 I'm sure we .... to cook anything for them because they .... lunch before they come here.

7 When people asked Gina's dad if he had children, his typical answer .... "And how!" Her mother usually murmured, "I wish he .... things like that."

Modals of deduction, obligation, and advice

Deduction: **must**, **have to**, **have got to**, **can't**, and **couldn't**

We use **must** to say that a particular idea or deduction is very likely or certain, based on the evidence (1).
We use **must** in the modal progressive for a deduction about what is happening now (2).

   1 *You're shivering—you **must** be cold.* • *Look at that car! Ali's parents **must** have a lot of money!*
   2 *Listen. It **must be raining** outside.* • *I think I **must be getting** the flu.* (NOT ~~I must get the flu.~~)

We use **must** plus the perfect when we want to express a deduction about what has already happened (3)
and when we report deductions in clauses after past tense verbs (4).

   3 *Someone **must have taken** the key because it isn't here.* (NOT ~~Someone must take the key.~~)
   4 *We realized he **must have lied**.* • *I thought at first that someone **must have made** a mistake.*
We use **must** in indirect speech when the information is still true: *He said she **must** be Italian.*

We can also use **have to** or **have got to** instead of **must** for a deduction in informal situations.

   5 *I didn't order 10 books. This **has to** be a mistake.* • *These aren't mine—they**'ve got to** be yours.*

We use **can't** or **couldn't** (not **must not**) as the opposite of **must** in negative deductions (6). We use
can't or **couldn't** plus the perfect for negative deductions about earlier events (7).

   6 *The bill is over $50—that **can't** be right.* • *You **can't** be 21!* (NOT ~~You must not be 21!~~)
   7 *You **can't have finished** already!* • *If he wasn't there, he **couldn't have committed** the murder.*

A Choose an ending (a–e) for each beginning (1–5) and add appropriate forms of *must* or *can't*.

1 Julia goes to Mexico every summer. (...)	a She .... in school yet.
2 What she's asking for is ridiculous. (...)	b If one is correct, the other .... be.
3 The hands on the clock weren't moving. (...)	c It's crazy. She .... joking.
4 Their daughter turned three this year. (...)	d She .... really like it there.
5 Those are two contradictory statements. (...)	e It .... stopped working.

B Complete the dialogue with *must* or *couldn't* plus appropriate forms of these verbs.

be, carry, do, lose, put, take

Ms. Tan (putting on her coat): I'm going to have to go down to the bakery for more bread.
Alan: Why?
Ms. Tan: I'm not sure what happened. I made some sandwiches earlier and left them on the table
          when I went to answer the phone. But someone (1) .... them
          because they're gone.
Alan: Oh, it (2) .... Dad. I'm sure he was in the kitchen earlier.
Ms. Tan: No, he left for his tennis match before I finished making them, so he
          (3) .... it. Anyway, he (4) .... a plate of
          sandwiches as well as all his tennis stuff, so I'm sure it wasn't him.
Alan   (opening fridge door): Well, it wasn't me. But Mom—look! Are these your sandwiches
          here on the bottom shelf of the fridge?
Ms. Tan: Are they in there? Oh, my goodness. I (5) .... them in there when
          the phone rang. Oh, dear. I really (6) .... my mind. Now, why did
          I put on my coat?

Obligation and advice: **should**

We use **should** to express an obligation (8), to describe what is expected (9), and generally to say what we think is a good or appropriate idea (10).

   8 *The police **should** crack down on speeding. • At election time, everyone **should** vote.*

   9 *You're a student. You **should** be studying! • Nurses and doctors **shouldn't** smoke.*

  10 *Teachers **should** get better salaries. • Children **should** learn to say "Please" and "Thank you."*

We use **should** when we ask for and give advice (11) or warnings (12).

  11 *What **should** I do? • You **should** take notes during lectures. • You **should** get to the airport early.*

  12 *You **shouldn't** go swimming right after eating. • You **shouldn't** walk through the park at night.*

We can use **should** to say that something is likely because we have planned it or expect it.

  13 *If all goes well, we **should** be there before it gets dark. • The bus **should** come soon.*

We use **should** plus the perfect when we think that something good or desirable did not happen (14), often as a way of expressing regret (15).

  14 *They **should have rehearsed** before playing. • We **should have left** a tip for our waiter.*

  15 *We **should have been** more careful with our money. • I **shouldn't have told** anyone about it.*

Obligation and advice: **ought to**, **be supposed to**, and **had better**

We can use **ought to** instead of **should** with no difference in meaning.

  16 *Neighbours **ought to/should** help each other. • You really **ought to/should** be more careful. • He **should/ought to** have completed the work before he left.* (NOT ~~He ought have completed the work.~~)

The negative is **ought not to**: *You ought not to wait.* (NOT ~~You ought not wait.~~)

We can also use **be supposed to** instead of **should**, usually in informal situations (17). We can use **be supposed to** (not **should**) when we report what others think is true (18).

  17 *You **are supposed to/should** be sleeping.* (NOT ~~You supposed to be sleeping.~~)

  18 *Killing a spider **is supposed to** be unlucky.* (NOT ~~Killing a spider should be unlucky.~~)

We can use **had better** as a stronger version of **should** when we recommend (19) or warn against (20) doing something.

  19 *You have failed two tests. You **had better** start working harder or you won't pass the course.*

  20 *Miguel's going to take your bike. ~ He'**d better not** do that!* (NOT ~~He'd not better do that.~~)

C Add these nouns and verbs to the sentences.

cricket, mirror, shoulder, had better, ought not, should be, ladders, person, umbrella, is supposed to, shouldn't, should have

If you listen to the advice of a superstitious (1) ...., you (2) ....
be ready to pay a lot of attention to what you're doing each day. Be careful with that
(3) .... You'll be told that you (4) .... open it indoors. When you're
walking along the street, watch out for (5) .... You (6) .... careful not
to walk under one. Did you spill any salt recently? You know that you (7) ....
immediately thrown some of it over your (8) ...., don't you? And remember that you
(9) .... to be careless with a (10) ...., because if you break one, you'll
have seven years of bad luck. However, if you see a (11) ...., that's good, because it
(12) .... be lucky.

Negatives and questions

Negatives are usually formed with an auxiliary verb (**be, do,** or **have**) or a modal plus **not**/**n't** before the main verb (*I **am not** crying, you **don't** care, he **hasn't** gone, we **shouldn't** wait*).

Questions are usually formed with an auxiliary verb (**be, do,** or **have**) or a modal before the subject and the main verb (***Has** he gone? **Should** we wait?*).

There are yes/no questions (***Are** you crying? **Do** they care?*) and **wh**-questions (***Where has** he gone? **Why should** we wait?*).

A Read through this text and find

1 another yes/no question
2 the one sentence that contains two negative verbs

A **Why did you start the "Protect Yourself" program?** A good friend of mine was robbed last year on her way home from work. She wasn't seriously injured, but it really frightened her and she wouldn't go out alone. I started talking to her about protecting herself and she thought it would be a good idea to form a group. Eventually we had so many people that it turned into a regular kind of night class.

B **Who can take part?** Anyone who wants to, but mostly it's young women. We meet in an old building that's next to the big church on Wilder Avenue, from 6 to 7 on Mondays.

C **Do you teach karate and stuff like that?** Not really. We tried some of that at first, but it wasn't very successful. There is a real karate class in the same building on Thursdays for people who want that. We still use some of the movements from karate when we talk about ways to escape, but we focus more on not getting into that kind of situation.

D **What do you mean? How do you not get into "that kind of situation"?** We talk a lot about not becoming a victim and thinking of ways to avoid being attacked. It's really more about awareness and how not to be an easy target. There are some statistics about assault victims that we talk about. For example, women with longer hair are more likely to be attacked than women whose hair is shorter or in a style that can't be grabbed.

E **Is there anything else?** Clothing is another thing. Women in skirts and dresses are attacked more than those wearing jeans or pants.

F **When and where do most attacks occur?** At night, of course. But surprisingly, a large number of assaults occur in the early morning, before 8:30. They happen in isolated areas, parks, outside schools and office buildings before and after regular working hours. We advise women not to go alone to parking areas and garages in the morning or in the evening. But, if you must, you should carry an umbrella or something like that and, if you're going to your car, have your keys ready.

G **What's the umbrella for? Is it a weapon?** Well, it isn't much of a weapon, is it? But we think it helps you feel more confident. We actually practise using the umbrella to keep someone at a distance while you shout and scream as loud as you can to discourage any attacker who wants you to be an easy victim.

H **What should you do if you're actually attacked?** Be a problem. Grab fingers and bend them backwards. Bite hands. Stomp your foot down hard on the attacker's toes. Grab the skin under the arm above the attacker's elbow and squeeze as hard as you can. Move, twist, kick, scratch, fall down, scream, and yell. Be hard to hold and make a lot of noise.

B Choose one of the following as the final sentence of the last five paragraphs above (D–H)

1 We want you to be a difficult problem. (...)
2 Maybe that's why there are also more attacks in warmer weather. (...)
3 You may be fighting for your life. (...)
4 It isn't wise to stand out there searching for something in your purse. (...)
5 A ponytail can make you very vulnerable. (...)

Word order in negatives

With auxiliaries **be** and **have** and modals, we form negatives with **not/n't.** In formal situations we use the full form (**We are not**) (1). In informal situations, we usually contract **not** (**We aren't**) (2) or we contract the auxiliary (**We're not**) and the modal (**We'll not**) (3).

1 *Dogs **are not** allowed off their leashes.* • *Guests **must not** eat or drink outside.*
2 *They **aren't** listening.* • *We **haven't** forgotten the meeting.* • *Her parents **won't** let her go.*
3 *We're **not** ready yet.* • *I've **not** been given any instructions.*

With other verbs, we form negatives with **do** plus **not/n't** before the base form of the verb.

4 *Some people **do not** understand.* • *It **does not** work.* • *I **did not** refuse to pay.* • *They **don't** remember.* • *It **doesn't** help us.* • *We **didn't** see it.* (NOT ~~We didn't saw it.~~)

Negative forms of **do** are not used with modal verbs: *I **can't** swim.* (NOT ~~I don't can swim.~~)

In sentences with infinitives and gerunds, we put **not** before the infinitive or gerund.

5 *He pretended **not to see** us.* • *I enjoyed **not going** to school for a few days.*

We can use **no** before nouns (6), and negative adverbs such as **no longer** or **never** before verbs (7).

6 *There were **no** problems.* • *We'll have **no** money for rent.* (NOT ~~We'll no have money for rent.~~)
7 *She's **no longer** working there.* • *They will **never** be free.* (NOT ~~They will be never free.~~)

Word order in questions

With auxiliaries **be** and **have** and modals, we form questions by putting the auxiliary or modal before the subject. We put the main verb after the subject.

8 ***Are you** coming?* • ***Have they** finished?* • *Why **must you** leave?* (NOT ~~Why you must leave?~~) • *How **can I** help?* • *Where **was your watch** made?* (NOT ~~Where was made your watch?~~)

With other verbs, we form questions with **do** before the subject and the base form of the verb.

9 ***Do you** know the answer?* • *What **does she** want?* • ***Did he** break it?* (NOT ~~Did he broke it?~~)

We begin yes/no questions with **be, do, have,** or a modal and usually use them to get **Yes** or **No** as an answer (10). We can use yes/no questions joined by **or** when we offer a choice between two possible answers (11).

10 ***Am I** the first to arrive?* • ***Are you** feeling okay?* • ***Do you** like it?* • ***Does it** work?* • ***Have you** got a minute?* • ***Has it** stopped raining?* • ***May we** come in?* • ***Can you** play the piano?*
11 *Do we go now **or** wait until later?* • *Would you like something hot **or** something cold to drink?*

Wh-questions begin with **wh**-words (question words) and ask for specific information.

12 ***What's** your name?* • ***How much** does it cost?* • ***When** and **where** you play hockey?*
Other **wh**-words include **which, who, whom, whose, why**

When we use **what** or **who** as the subject, we usually put the main verb (not **do**) after them.

13 ***What's making** that noise?* • ***Who used** my computer?* (NOT ~~Who did use my computer?~~)
Note similar uses of **whose** and **which** with nouns: ***Whose** phone is ringing?* • ***Which** team won?*

C **Find one sentence containing an example of each of the following in the text on page 16.**

1 A negative modal: ....
2 A negative infinitive: ....
3 A negative gerund: ....
4 A **wh**-word used as subject: ....

Negative questions and question tags

Negative questions

Negative yes/no questions usually begin with negative forms of **be**, **do**, **have**, or a modal (1). In negative **wh**-questions, we put the negative forms after the **wh**-words (2).

    1 *Aren't those books mine?* • *Doesn't he speak any English?* • *Didn't she get married last year?* • *Hasn't the lecture finished yet?* • *Haven't we seen that movie?* • *Can't you open the window?*

    2 *Everyone was invited to the party.* • *Why **didn't** you go?* (NOT ~~Why you didn't go?~~) • *There are only 10 players on the field.* • *Who **isn't** here yet?* (NOT ~~Who isn't he here yet?~~)

When we answer negative yes/no questions, we use **Yes** to say the positive is true and **No** to say the negative is true.

    3 *Aren't they Quebecois?* *Yes.* (= They are Quebecois.) *No.* (= They aren't Quebecois.)

We put negative adverbs such as **never** and emphatic **not** after the subject (not the auxiliary) in negative questions.

    4 *Have you **never** eaten meat?* • *Did he **not** understand the text?* (NOT ~~Did not he understand the text?~~)

We can use negative yes/no questions to ask for confirmation (5) or to express surprise (6).

    5 *Isn't July 1st a big Canadian holiday?* • *Haven't we already paid for the tickets?*

    6 *Doesn't she like any music at all?* • *Haven't you ever seen snow?*

Questions beginning with **Why don't you …?** or **Why not …?** are used for offers or suggestions.

    7 *Why don't you come with us?* • *Why not have the party on Saturday instead of Friday?*
There is no subject after **Why not …?** (NOT ~~Why not you have the party on Saturday?~~)

Question tags

Question tags are short forms of questions added after statements. We usually use a positive statement + negative tag (8) or a negative statement + positive tag (9).

    8 *We're late, **aren't we**?* • *Philippe really loves her, **doesn't he**?* • *She lost it, **didn't she**?*

    9 *I can't win, **can I**?* • *They don't like it, **do they**?* • *You haven't studied at all, **have you**?*
The full forms (**are we not?**, **does he not?**) are very formal.

In question tags, we use a pronoun that matches the subject of the sentence and a verb that matches the main verb auxiliary (if there is one) or **be** (as a main verb), or we use a form of **do**.

    10 *You **haven't** talked to Maricel since she went on vacation, **have you**?* (NOT ~~didn't she?~~)
         *He **was** guilty, **wasn't he**?* • *The evidence **showed** he was guilty, **didn't it**?* (NOT ~~wasn't he?~~)
Note that we use a positive tag with **they** after **no one** or **nobody**: *Nobody likes it, do they?*

We use modals in tags after imperatives for requests or proposals.

    11 *Don't say anything, **will you**?* • *Pass me that knife, **could you**?* • *Let's leave, **shall we**?*

We can use a positive tag after a positive sentence when we want to confirm information, often after repeating what a previous speaker said. A negative tag after a negative sentence is very rare.

    12 *That's your new car, **is it**?* • *So, the students are planning a protest, **are they**?*

A Find one example of each of the following in the text on page 16.

1 a negative question: ....

2 a sentence with a question tag: ....

B Using a dictionary if necessary, complete the sentences with these words.

isn't, doesn't, no, nondescript, non-refundable, non-stick, aren't, won't, not, non-event, non-resident, non-stop

1 There usually .... any problems washing a pan if it's the .... kind.
2 When someone .... living permanently in a country, he or she is a

   ....
3 If something is expected to be big or dramatic, but it's ...., it can be described as

   a ....
4 .... means the money won't be returned, ... it?
5 The word .... is used for something which has .... special or
   unusual features.
6 If your trip is ...., you .... be able to visit any of the places along
   the way.

C Complete the questions with these words.

What, Where, Whose, When, Who, Why, are, do, isn't, did, don't, were

1 I have 20 names and only 19 students. .... here today?
2 We have an extra room in our place. .... you stay with us?
3 Everyone was looking for Mr. Hum. .... you tell them he was?
4 There must be hundreds of people working there. .... they all do?
5 Your parents worked in Saudi Arabia? .... they there?
6 Some things were left in the classroom yesterday. .... books .... these?

D Correct the mistakes in the use of negatives and questions in this text.

In our group, we had to write down questions before a discussion of the topic "What kind of pet is

best?" That was difficult because some of us ~~didn't~~ ever had a pet, so we didn't really could say much

about this topic. I asked Michel, "What you think is the best pet?" He answered, "I not care about

pets." Then he said, "Why we have pets? We not need them for anything, don't we? And some people

think dogs not clean, so they not good pets." I asked him, "Aren't some pets cleaner than dogs? For

example, no one thinks a cat makes more mess than a dog, does he?" He didn't answered. Then Paola

explained that she could have not a cat in her house because cats made her mother sneeze a lot.

So she suggested that an important question was: "Why do some people can't have pets?" I wrote

down three other questions from our group: "Do some pets more expensive to keep than others?"

"How will be trained the pet?" "Who is take care of the pet?"

(handwritten above "didn't ever": hadn't)

Negative words

No, none, nobody, no one, and nothing

Although we normally use negative verbs (**wasn't**, **haven't**) to express negative concepts (1), we can also use positive verbs with negative words such as **no**, **none**, **nobody**, **no one**, and **nothing** (2). We can use these negative words as subjects with positive verbs (3).

    1 *There **wasn't** anything to eat in the hotel room, so we **haven't** had breakfast yet.*
    2 *There was **nothing** to eat in the hotel room, so **none** of us has had breakfast yet.*
    3 ***No one** complained. • **Nobody** told us.* (NOT ~~Not anybody told us.~~ / ~~Nobody didn't tell us.~~)

We use **no** before nouns and **none** instead of nouns.

    4 *Didn't you bring any money? ~ I have **no** money. / I have **none**.* (NOT ~~I have none money.~~)
We don't normally use double negatives. (NOT ~~I don't have no money.~~ / ~~I don't have none.~~)

    We use **none of** before pronouns and determiners (**the, those, our**, etc.).
    5 ***None of them** understood it. • **None of our** friends will come. • **None of the** lights is working.*

We can use **no** with both singular and plural nouns or a gerund to emphasize the negative. We can use this structure instead of a negative verb (6) or as a shorthand for "is / are not allowed" in formal situations (7).

    6 *One class doesn't have a teacher.* → *One class has **no** teacher.*
      Cameras aren't permitted inside the court. → ***No** cameras are permitted inside the court.*
    7 ***No** dogs. **No** skateboards. • **No** talking during the examination. • **No** parking.*
We use **Don't** + verb rather than **No** + gerund in informal situations: *Don't park there.*

We can use **no** or **not /n't any** with comparative adjectives (8) and adverbs (9).

    8 *These seats are **no better** than the others. / These seats are**n't any better** than the others.*
    9 *We should leave **no later** than 8:30. / We should**n't** leave **any later** than 8:30.*

We use **not** rather than **no** in reduced negatives (10), before the indefinite article **a /an** (11), and before quantifiers such as **all** or **a lot** (12).

    10 *Do you want to keep these boxes **or not**? **If not**, I'll just throw them out.*
    11 ***Not a** single drop was spilled. • A whale is a mammal, **not a** fish.*
    12 ***Not all** lawyers are rich. • There is **not a lot** to be gained by being rude to people.*

Inversion after negative words and phrases

We use inversion after negative adverbs such as **never** or **nowhere** when they are placed in front position for emphasis. We put the subject after an auxiliary verb (**be, do, have**) or a modal.

    13 *I have never heard such nonsense.* → *Never **have I** heard such nonsense.*
      They couldn't find a bottle opener anywhere. → *Nowhere **could they** find a bottle opener.*

We also use inversion after negative phrases with **no** (14) and **not** (15) in front position.

    14 *The children weren't in danger at any time.* → *At no time **were the children** in danger.*
      You shouldn't go under any circumstances. → *Under no circumstances **should you** go.*
    15 *I didn't realize what she meant until later.* → *Not until later **did I** realize what she meant.*
      Marcia is not only single, but she is also rich. → *Not only **is Marcia** single, but she is also rich.*

Inversion is typically used in formal or literary English, but we can also use it in informal replies, after **neither, nor,** and **no way.**

    16 *I don't understand. ~ Neither **do I**. • We didn't like the movie. ~ Nor **did most people**. • I think Mr. Zirnis should let us leave early. ~ No way **will he** agree to that.*

A Choose an ending (a–d) for each beginning (1–4) and add *no*, *none*, or *not*.

1 I wrote to several people, (...)
2 We needed some glue, (...)
3 .... food is allowed in that room, (...)
4 There's .... much money left (...)

a so you must .... eat in there.
b and we have .... traveller's cheques.
c but .... of them has replied yet.
d but there was .... in the house.

B Using a dictionary if necessary, complete the sentences with these words.

carefree, indifferent, infrequent, careless, infallible, invisible, doesn't, no, not, never, no one, nothing

If something is (1) ...., it (2) .... happen very often.

When you are (3) ...., you have (4) .... to worry about, but the word
(5) .... isn't the same. It means (6) .... paying enough attention to detail.

An object is (7) .... if (8) .... can see it.

If people or things are (9) ...., they (10) .... make mistakes or go wrong.

When people are (11) .... to something, they have (12) .... interest in it.

C Rewrite these sentences in a more informal style.

▶ Nowhere else do they make this bread. *They don't make this bread anywhere else.*

1 Never has there been a better chance to make money on the stock market.

....

2 Not until the next morning did we notice that she had not come home.

....

3 At no time did anyone warn us about polluted water.

....

4 The janitor will say, "No smoking in here," will he not?

....

D Complete the text with these words and phrases.

no idea, not only, nor, no sooner, not until, nothing, did I, had I, were they, did we, I had, they were

Have you ever arrived at work thinking something was wrong? It recently happened to me. On
Saturday morning, when I arrived at the City Concert Hall, there were a lot of musicians waiting
outside. (1) .... (2) .... opened the front door than the musicians
started to come in and complain. (3) .... (4) .... unhappy that their
next concert had been cancelled, but (5) .... also very angry that they hadn't been
paid for weeks. I tried to explain that I only looked after the Concert Hall and (6) ....
(7) .... to do with money or music. They said that a lot of tickets had been sold,
but they had (8) .... where the money had gone. (9) ....
(10) ...., I kept telling them. (11) .... two days later
(12) .... all find out that the concert organizer had run off with all the money.

Question words

What or which?

We can use **what** and **which** before nouns or as pronouns (1). We use **what** when we think there is an unlimited number of possible answers (2) and **which** when we think there is a limited number (3).

1 *What bus/which bus should I take?* • *What/Which do you want?*
2 *What are you doing?* • *What's her home phone number?* • *What would you like to drink?*
3 *There are three numbers listed here.* ***Which** is her home phone number?* • *We have both red wine and white wine.* ***Which** would you prefer?*

We use **which** (not **what**) before **one** or **ones** (4). We use **which of** (not **what of**) before determiners (**the, this, my,** etc.) (5) and pronouns (6) when we ask about things and people in a limited set.

4 *There are a lot of cups of coffee here.* ***Which ones** already have sugar?* ***Which one** is mine?*
5 ***Which of** these books haven't you read?* (NOT ~~What of these books haven't you read?~~)
6 *Keilberg had four sons.* ***Which (one) of** them was the famous artist?* • ***Which of** you is first?*

We can use **who** to ask a general question: **Who is first?** (NOT ~~Who of you is first?~~)

A Choose a question (a–f) to follow each statement (1–6) and add *What* or *Which*.

1 I'm one of the girls in that old photo. (...)
2 "Bob's your uncle!" is a British phrase. (...)
3 He gave us our test results. (...)
4 I'd like to leave soon. (...)
5 I got 19 out of 20 correct. (...)
6 I haven't read all his books. (...)

a .... was your score?
b .... one did you get wrong?
c .... are you waiting for?
d .... is you?
e .... of them have you read?
f .... does it mean?

Question words with prepositions and adverbs

We can use **wh-**questions to ask about the objects of prepositions. We usually put the preposition at the end of a **wh-**question (7). In formal uses, the preposition is sometimes put at the beginning (8).

7 *He's going to fill the hole with something.* → ***What** is he going to fill the hole **with**?*
You gave your old computer to someone. → ***Whom** did you give your old computer **to**?*
8 ***With what** is he going to fill the hole?* • ***To whom** did you give your old computer?*

In some **wh-**questions (**What ... for?, What/Who ...like?**), the preposition is always at the end.

9 *What are you doing that **for**?* • *Whom does she look **like**?* (NOT ~~Like whom does she look?~~)

There are some prepositions that we use at the beginning (not the end) of **wh-**questions.

10 ***During which** period was this a French colony?* • ***Since when** have these records been kept?*
Other prepositions used like this include **above, after, before, below**

We usually put adverbs after **wh-**words (11), but we can use some adverbs before **wh-**words (12).

11 ***How often** do you exercise?* • ***What else** did he say?* • ***When exactly** did he leave Yellowknife?*
12 ***Precisely where** did you last see the keys?* • ***Exactly when** did he leave Yellowknife?*

Wh-words with **ever** (such as **wherever, whoever**) are used to express surprise or disbelief.

13 ***Wherever** did you find that?* • ***However** did she do it?* • ***Whoever** told you such nonsense?*
We don't use **whichever** in this way: ***Whatever** do you mean?* (NOT ~~Whichever do you mean?~~)

B Complete the quiz questions with these words, then try to choose the correct answers.

by, for, how, often, where, who, with, during, from (×2), of, what (×2), which (×2), whom

1 . . . . century did the French Revolution begin? (. .)
(A) 17th (B) 18th (C) 19th

2 . . . . does an annual meeting take place? (. .)
(A) every week (B) every month (C) every year

3 Cider is a type of drink. . . . . is it made . . . . ? (. .)
(A) apples (B) grapes (C) oranges

4 . . . . did Paul McCartney write many of the Beatles' hit songs? (. .)
(A) Mick Jagger (B) Elton John (C) John Lennon

5 . . . . these countries is not in South America? (. .)
(A) Bolivia (B) Nicaragua (C) Paraguay

6 Hugh Jackman is a well-known actor. . . . . is he . . . . ? (. .)
(A) Australia (B) Canada (C) Scotland

7 *Barney's Version* is the title of a famous book. . . . . was it written
. . . . ? (. .)
(A) Margaret Atwood (B) Stephen Leacock (C) Mordecai Richler

8 . . . . is a whisk used . . . . ? (. .)
(A) beating cattle, horses, etc. (B) playing cellos, violins, etc. (C) stirring eggs, cream, etc.

C Complete the dialogue with these words and phrases.

how ever, what … about, where, where … from, who, how long, whatever, where exactly,
which … in, who else

The phone woke me up. I automatically reached over and picked it up.

"Good morning, darling. I guess you're not coming to get me, are you?"

"What? (1) . . . . is this?"

"It's me. Charles. (2) . . . . were you expecting?"

"Sorry. I'm still asleep. Aren't you in Montreal?"

"(3) . . . . are you talking . . . . ? (4) . . . . gave you that idea?"

"You're not? Oh, no, I can't think straight. (5) . . . . are you?"

"I'm at the airport. I just got back from San Jose."

"Oh, goodness. (6) . . . . have you been waiting? I'm so sorry."

"It's okay. Don't panic. I'm just about to pick up my luggage."

"I'm up. I'll be there. (7) . . . . are you? (8) . . . . terminal are you
. . . . ?"

"It's okay. I'll catch the bus downtown. Can you meet me at the station?"

"Yes. It'll be faster that way. I'll see you in about 45 minutes."

"Okay. Bye."

I started to put the phone down, but there was something wet and sticky on it. Was it blood?
(9) . . . . had it come . . . . ? There was more of it on the sheet.
(10) . . . . did it get there?

Other question types

Questions inside questions

We can put a yes/no question asking what people think (1) or say (2) after the **wh**-word (**what, who**) inside a **wh**-question.

    1 *Do you think something is wrong?* → *What **do you think** is wrong?*
      (NOT *What you think is wrong?*)
    2 *Did he say someone was waiting outside?* → *Who **did he say** was waiting outside?*

When we put a yes/no question inside a **wh**-question, we use question word order in the yes/no question, not in the **wh**-question.

    3 *Does he believe the fighting will end?* → *When **does he believe** the fighting will end?*
      (NOT *When does he believe will the fighting end?*)

Statements used as questions

We can use a statement as a yes/no question to ask for confirmation of something (4) or to repeat what was just said, usually to express surprise (5). We can use a **wh**-word in a statement to ask for clarification or to get more information about part of what was just said (6).

    4 *Monday **is** a holiday?* • *Mr. Li **was** your teacher too?* • *David **doesn't** know about this?*
    5 *Erdem won first prize.* ~ ***He won first prize?*** • *I had a ticket, but didn't go.* ~ ***You didn't go?***
    6 *She zapped it.* ~ *She **did what to** it?* • *I met Yvonne.* ~ *You met **who?*** (NOT *Did you meet who?*)

Rhetorical questions

Rhetorical questions have the form of a question, but can be used to assert something (7). We can use rhetorical questions to establish a topic (8), or to highlight a previous question (9) before giving an answer.

    7 *Miguel isn't here yet.* ~ ***Who cares?*** (= I don't care.) ***Isn't he always late?*** (= He is always late.)
    8 ***Do you remember Y2K?*** *We were sure then that the computers would all fail.*
    9 *What do you think of it?* ~ ***What do I think of it?*** *I think it's just too expensive.*

Reduced questions

In informal situations, yes/no questions are sometimes used without **Are you?** or **Do /Did you?** (10) and **wh**-questions can be reduced to the **wh**-word alone (11) or short phrases (12).

    10 *Feeling okay?* • *Tired?* • *Going out?* • *Need some help?* • *Like it?* • *Have fun last night?*
    11 *We must buy that piano.* ~ ***How?*** ~ *I'll find the money.* ~ ***Where?*** ~ *I know someone.* ~ ***Who?***
    12 *You have to do it.* ~ ***Why me?*** • *Your plan won't work.* ~ ***Why not?*** • *Bring a knife.* ~ ***What for?***

We also use the phrases **How about?** (13) and **What about?** (14) without verbs before nouns and gerunds to make suggestions or to draw attention to something.

    13 ***How about** a cup of coffee?* • ***How about** watching TV?* (NOT *How about shall we watch TV?*)
    14 ***What about** your homework?* • ***What about** playing crokinole?* (NOT *What about we play crokinole?*)

Indirect questions

We use indirect questions when we report what was asked. We don't use question word order or a question mark in indirect questions (15). We begin indirect yes/no questions with **if** or **whether** (16).

    15 *Why did you start the movie?* → *I asked her **why** she (had) started the movie.*
      What do you mean? → *I asked her **what** she meant.* (NOT *I asked her what did she mean?*)
    16 *Do you teach karate?* → *I asked **if** they taught karate.* (NOT *I asked did they teach karate?*)
      Is it an umbrella or a weapon? → *I asked **whether** it was an umbrella or a weapon.*

A Rewrite these statements as questions beginning with *What*, *When*, *Where*, and *Who*.

▶ They think something is wrong. ....What do they think is wrong?....

1 You believe someone is responsible for the current conflict.

....

2 Her father thought she might have gone somewhere.

....

3 The weather forecaster said the rain should stop at some time.

....

4 You imagine their new house is going to look like something.

....

B Choose a question (a–e) to follow each beginning (1–5) and add these words.

did, didn't, do, does, how, which, who, why

1 Will it be sunny tomorrow? (...)
2 Olga, you have to crawl through the tunnel. (...)
3 I understood nothing he said. (...)
4 I don't know how I'll pass the exam. (...)
5 He says there is a problem with the contract. (...)

a .... he? With .... part?
b .... about studying?
c .... knows?
d You .... ? Neither .... I!
e .... I have to? .... me?

C The dialogue takes place in a police station between Ms. McCord and Detective Kapur. Complete it with these words.

he did, he's, he was, I do, you're, you don't, did he, is he, was he, do I, are you, don't you

"Can we leave now or (1) .... going to start paying us for all the time we're spending here?"

"Your son isn't going anywhere, Ms. McCord. (2) .... in deep trouble this time."

"(3) .... really? Maybe you're the one who's in trouble, detective. My son has done nothing. This is police harassment."

"I asked your son what (4) .... doing in John Mansfield's house last night and what do you think he said?"

"What (5) .... think? I think (6) .... making all this up because (7) .... have a clue. You're just trying to blame my Robbie for something he didn't do. He worked for Mr. Mansfield. That's all."

"Listen. I didn't tell your son that Mansfield was killed with a knife. He told me. He wasn't just helping us make this up, (8) .... ?"

"Oh, (9) .... make you think he was going to confess? I don't know what you think (10) .... One thing (11) .... know for sure is that he was at home with me all last night. Why (12) .... just leave him alone and go find the real killer?"

Passives with modals, infinitives, and gerunds

Modal passives

We form simple modal passives with a modal (**can, may, will**, etc.) + **be** + a past participle (1).
We use **could, might, would** + **be** + a past participle when we need to use a past tense (2).
  1 *The police will arrest violent demonstrators. So, if you are violent, you **will be arrested**.*
    *You **can be kept** in custody for 24 hours and you **may be questioned** about your activities.*
  2 *"The police can't stop us!" The demonstrators claimed that they **couldn't be stopped**.*
    *They boasted that although they **might be arrested**, they **wouldn't be silenced**.*

We form modal perfect passives with a modal + **have been** + past participle.
  3 *Tony didn't study for the test. His answers **must have been copied** from someone else.*
    *If he had been caught cheating, he **would have been expelled** from school.*

We can form modal progressive passives with a modal + **be being** + past participle (4). We rarely
use these passives. Instead, we use an active or a progressive passive without a modal (5).
  4 *I see that someone is working on the roof today. I think it **may be being repaired** at last.*
  5 *Perhaps they're repairing it at last. • I think it's being repaired at last.*

We form phrasal modal passives with the present (6) or past (7) of a phrasal modal such as
be going to or **have to** + **be** + past participle. We can use two phrasal modals together (8).
  6 *Someone has to tell Jodi to stop interrupting. → Jodi **has to be told** to stop interrupting.*
    *Are you going to need this extra paper? → Is this extra paper **going to be needed**?*
  7 *I had to find a place for all the boxes. → A place **had to be found** for all the boxes.*
    *Someone was probably going to steal them. → They **were** probably **going to be stolen**.*
  8 *We're going to have to sell my old car. → My old car **is going to have to be sold**.*

Passive infinitives and gerunds

We use **to be** + past participle for the passive infinitive (9) and **to have been** + past participle for
the perfect passive infinitive (10).
  9 *He's trying to finish the work soon. He expects most of it **to be finished** before the weekend.*
  10 *They have chosen Bhairavi Mehra to play the part. She's really excited **to have been chosen**.*

We use **being** + past participle for the passive gerund (11) and **having been** + past participle for
the perfect passive gerund (12).
  11 *He was asking about a lot of personal things. I didn't like **being asked** about my private life.*
  12 *I think they've promoted Ramy, but he didn't mention **having been promoted** when we talked.*

We put **not** before passive infinitives (13) and passive gerunds (14) to form negatives.
  13 *They didn't invite us. It was strange **not to be invited**.* (NOT … ~~to be not invited.~~)
  14 *No one had informed me about that. I resented **not having been informed**.*

A **Complete the sentences with *be*, *to be*, *being*, or *been* and decide what type of passive
each one is.**

  1 After .... trapped for hours, the miners were found alive. (...)   a Simple modal passive
  2 I've looked for the students, but they are nowhere .... seen. (...)   b Modal perfect passive
  3 Medical teams have had to .... flown in to some remote areas. (...)   c Passive gerund
  4 The books seem to have .... stolen. (...)   d Phrasal modal passive
  5 If the dog returns, our cats may .... scared away. (...)   e Passive infinitive
  6 The hikers could have .... lost out in the woods. (...)   f Perfect passive infinitive

B Complete the news report with these verbs in the passive.

block, close, destroy, expect, flood, injure, knock, leave, report, rescue

Many homes on the island of Jamaica (1) .... by hurricane Lester yesterday. Today, high winds (2) .... to bring more rain and problems for the island's residents. Some parts of the island (3) .... without electricity last night and many roads (4) .... by fallen trees that (5) .... down during the storm. The area around Savanna-La-Mar on the south coast (6) .... and some residents have had (7) .... from the roofs of their houses.

   Most businesses and schools in Kingston (8) .... today as people emerge from their battered homes to survey the damage. More than 100 people (9) .... , but no deaths (10) ....

C Complete each sentence with a passive so that it has a similar meaning to the one above.

1 You can't see the house from the street.
   The house ....

2 "They won't correct your papers before Friday."
   He said our papers ....

3 Someone must have taken the towels out of the dryer.
   The towels ....

4 Nobody's going to steal your books from this room.
   Your books ....

5 People were telling me what to do all the time and I didn't enjoy it.
   I didn't enjoy ....

D Choose one passive verb phrase for each space in these sentences (from a report on the use of DNA testing by the police).

is also called, has also been used, can be used, is believed, have been shown,
may have been convicted, was released, had been sentenced, would never have been solved

DNA is the chemical in the cells of plants and animals that carries inherited characteristics, or genetic information. DNA testing (1)... to identify each person as a unique individual on the basis of that genetic information. It (2)... "genetic fingerprinting." The results of DNA testing are accepted as evidence in cases where it (3)... that the wrong person (4)... of a crime.

   In recent years, more than 70 people (5)... to be innocent through DNA testing. Many of those people (6)... to life in prison. In one case, a man (7)... after 19 years in prison. DNA testing (8)... in some murder cases that (9)... without it.

Passives with **by**-phrases and **get**

Passives with **by**-phrases

An agent is the person or thing that does or causes an action. In active sentences, the agent is the subject (1). In passive sentences, we don't usually mention the agent. We can include the agent in a **by**-phrase after the verb when the meaning is not complete without it (2) or for emphasis and contrast (3). We don't usually include pronouns or nouns with a general meaning such as **people** in a **by**-phrase (4).

1 *Shakespeare wrote* Hamlet. *Many famous actors have played the title role.*
2 Hamlet *was written by Shakespeare.* (NOT ~~Hamlet was written.~~)
   The title role has been played by many famous actors. (NOT ~~The title role has been played.~~)
3 *Was the Mona Lisa painted by Michelangelo or (by) Leonardo da Vinci?*
4 *We/People store equipment in the basement.* → *Equipment is stored in the basement.*

We can use a **by**-phrase for information about causes (5) and the method of doing something (6).

5 *The girl was bitten by a snake.* • *The flu is caused by a virus and can't be cured by antibiotics.*
6 *The temperature can be controlled by adjusting the thermostat.*

We use a **by**-phrase for the agent of an action and a **with**-phrase for the thing used to perform that action (7). After verbs such as **cover** or **decorate** used in the passive in descriptions, we typically use a **with**-phrase rather than a **by**-phrase (8).

7 *The rescue was recorded by a man <u>with a cellphone</u>.* • *The box was locked <u>with a gold key</u>.*
8 *Her costume was covered <u>with sparkles</u> and decorated <u>with rubies</u>.*
   (NOT ~~Her costume was decorated by rubies.~~)
Other verbs used in the passive plus **with** include **align, associate, crowd, fill**

A **Complete the sentences with appropriate forms of these verbs, plus *by* or *with* where necessary.**

The Globe

consider, establish, experience, fill, perform, not write

1 Shakespeare was born in 1564 and .... many to be the greatest English writer.
2 His early reputation .... writing and appearing in his own plays.
3 His plays .... interesting characters and memorable speeches.
4 Today, at the new Globe Theatre, the plays .... in conditions similar to those which .... audiences in Shakespeare's time.
5 Some people have claimed that many of the plays .... Shakespeare.

Passives with **get**

We can use **get** + past participle (9) instead of **be** + past participle (10) as a passive, usually in informal situations.

9 I'll **get paid** on Friday. • My books **got damaged** when the basement **got flooded** last year.

10 I'll **be paid** on Friday. • My books **were damaged** when the basement **was flooded** last year.

We use the auxiliary **do** in passives with **get** when we form questions or negatives.

11 Why **does** Javier **get asked** to go to all the parties? We **don't get invited** to any of them!

We often use passives with **get** for unexpected events (12) and difficult or bad experiences (13).

12 Professor Radic **got stuck** in traffic so her lecture **got moved** to later in the afternoon.

13 **Did** anyone **get injured?** Some people **got hurt.** They were lucky they **didn't get killed.**

Others like this include **get arrested, get broken, get caught, get divorced**

B **Choose an ending (a–d) for each beginning (1–4) and add these verbs.**

get beaten up, reacted, were reported, were stolen, get caught, was defeated, were smashed, were treated

1 After their team .... 2–0 on Wednesday night, (...)

2 Several store windows .... (...)

3 "Did any of the thieves .... ?" asked one store owner in frustration. (...)

4 Some people .... in the hospital for minor cuts and bruises, (...)

a but no serious injuries ...., according to the police.

b "Of course not," he explained. "Because nobody wants to .... by those hooligans."

c and items such as TVs, cellphones, and laptops ....

d angry hockey fans .... violently.

C **Add appropriate forms of these verbs to the text. Then in the space below, write those expressions (if any) that are used in the text to identify the agents of these verbs.**

carry, crash, hand, injure, knock, open, run, stop, ~~tell~~

When I was younger, people often (▶) ......told...... me that I was lucky. I remember one time, years ago, when I was sitting with friends in a large, crowded restaurant. The kitchen door suddenly (1) .... and a voice called out, "Fire! Get out!" Conversations (2) .... instantly as everyone and everything suddenly moved. Glasses and bottles (3) .... to the floor. As I started to get up from my seat, I (4) .... down. I struggled to my feet and then I (5) .... along by the surging crowd towards the door. I was pushed out of the door backwards by the force of the people behind me. Then I just (6) .... like everyone else until I reached a crowd at the end of the street. As I stood there waiting, a woman told me that there was blood on my cheek. I wiped the blood from my cheek with a piece of cloth that (7) .... to me by the woman. I thanked her. "It's just a scratch," she said. "You're lucky you didn't (8) .... seriously ...."

Agents: .people,..

....

Possessive and compound nouns

A **Write the numbers of appropriate examples in the spaces.**

Possessive noun or compound noun?

We usually use a possessive noun when something belongs to a particular person or thing ☐ and a compound noun to indicate a common combination of things, not possession ☐.
> 1 *Each **student's office** has a computer. • That red thing on a **chicken's head** is called a "comb."*
> 2 *You have to take these forms to the **student office**. • Do you like **chicken soup**?*

Possessive nouns

We form possessive nouns by adding an apostrophe **s** ('s) to most nouns, or only an apostrophe (') to plural nouns ending in s.
> 3 *one man's story, Lee's birthday, children's books, girls' stories*

Note that when a singular noun ends in **s**, we add an apostrophe **s** to form the possessive: *Don Coles's poems*

We use possessive noun phrases to express the idea of "having" (in a very general sense) which exists between the first noun and the second noun. We usually use them when the first noun refers to people and other living things ☐, groups and organizations ☐, times ☐, and places ☐.
> 4 *Montreal's night life, China's economic policy, Canada's currency, the world's population*
> 5 *My mother's sister, the Arcade Fire's music, the killer's mistake, a dog's life, birds' nests*
> 6 *the company's change of plan, the committee's decision, the CBC's programming*
> 7 *yesterday's meeting, next week's schedule, a week's pay, Monday's news*

We also use possessive nouns in personification, that is, when something abstract is treated as if it were a person ☐, or when an object is described as "having" something ☐.
> 8 *death's cold hand, love's passionate embrace, jealousy's dark thoughts*
> 9 *the car's previous owner, the computer's faulty design, the newspaper's circulation*

Possessive nouns can sometimes be used without a following noun when that noun is treated as known ☐, or is presented as one of a larger number rather than a particular one ☐.
> 10 *It's a film of Shelley Niro's. • She's a friend of Margaret.* (= one of Margaret's friends)
> 11 *She's at the doctor's. • We stayed at Hamut's. • It's bigger than Paul's.*

We can use an **of**-phrase after a noun to express "having," especially when one thing is part of another ☐, when describing actions, ideas, or processes ☐, or when a long phrase is used for the possessor ☐.
> 12 *the development **of** industry, the concerns **of** students, the withdrawal **of** NATO forces*
> 13 *the arm **of** the chair, pages **of** a book, the roof **of** the building, the cost **of** repairs*
> 14 *What was the name **of** that girl in Trout Lake? • He's the son **of** the woman we met in Wrigley.*

Compound nouns

Compound nouns consist of two (or more) words used to refer to people or things more specifically in terms of what they are for ☐, what they are made of ☐, what work they do ☐, what kind they are ☐, or where and when they happen or are used ☐. Some compound nouns are written with a hyphen or as a single word ☐.
> 15 *bus driver, car mechanic, history teacher, production manager, airline safety inspector*
> 16 *application form, can opener, fire extinguisher, swimming pool, emergency exit door*
> 17 *detective story, horror movie, junk food, independent contractor, fitness magazine*
> 18 *chicken soup, feather pillows, glass bottle, paper plates, vegetable filling*
> 19 *birthday party, morning sickness, street lights, winter coat, dining room table*
> 20 *a do-it-yourself store, a live-and-let-live approach, paperback, darkroom*

B Choose one expression from each pair for each blank line in this verse from a greeting card.

1 (Life's troubles / Troubles of life)
.... can sometimes leave us with a frown,

2 (each day's worries / worries of each day)
And the .... can get us down;

3 (morning special of news / morning's special news)
But this .... is here

4 (world's problems / worlds of the problems)
To make all the .... disappear;

5 (love's woman / woman's love)
Because of one ...., we can say

6 (Mother Day / Mother's Day)
Thanks and best wishes to you on this ....!

C Part A. Write these noun phrases in the appropriate spaces in the text.

application forms, consumer groups, credit rating, money matters, bottom line, credit card offers, giveaways, sense of responsibility, buy-now-pay-later world, credit cards, high-risk borrowers, T-shirts, college student, ~~credit card users,~~ interest rates

Part B. Find two possessive noun phrases with incorrect forms in this text and write correct versions here:

.... ; ....

Is your child starting school soon? Does he or she have a credit card yet? This isn't as strange as it sounds. According to Cathy Yuen, director of College Marketing Services in Los Angeles, (▶) _credit card users_ are getting younger and younger. You may be surprised to learn that teenagers have become one of the most important (1)..................................... In the US, those teens spend over $150 billion a year and an increasing amount of that spending is done with (2)...................................... For credit card companies, it has become crucial to establish a credit relationship with consumers as early as possible. That first credit card is the one that people are likely to keep using for the longest time. As a result, the typical (3)..................... receives over 40 (4)..................................... every year. Some lenders are now sending credit card (5)..................................... to high school students with offers of (6)..................................... such as free (7)...................................... Younger teens used to have to wait until they were 18 to sign a contract to get a card, but now their parents are co-signing. Credit card companies lose less money with teenagers than with adults, mainly because of parents willingness to help pay off their childrens credit card debt. Yuen says that, in terms of the (8)....................................., teens are not (9)...................................... There is also an advantage to getting an early start in the world of credit. If you establish a good (10)..................................... early on, you can get better (11)..................................... when you want to borrow money later for a car or a house. Teenagers may not be famous for their (12)..................................... when it comes to (13)....................................., but in this (14)....................................., they are learning at an early age how to get what they want by using plastic.

Articles and nouns in speech

New, old, and restated information

We use articles and nouns in different ways to help readers and listeners interpret information in speech. We introduce new information with **a / an** and repeat old information with **the**.

1 *At **a** public meeting this morning, **a** mayoral candidate announced **a** new proposal for **a** park downtown. **The** candidate hasn't yet provided any details about **the** park.*

2 *There was once **a** king of **a** faraway country who had **a** beautiful daughter. **The** king had searched **the** whole country to find a young prince to marry his daughter.*

3 *We read **a** report in **a** medical journal about **a** new treatment for asthma. **The** report said that **the** treatment had been effective, but was still experimental.*

We can use **the** plus a more general noun when old information is restated.

4 *After some questioning, **the** candidate admitted there were flaws in **the** proposal.*

5 ***The** beautiful **girl** was known throughout **the land** as "**the** lonely **princess**."*

6 *Soon after the report was released, **the news** of **the breakthrough** brought a barrage of phone calls from asthma sufferers.*

Writers sometimes begin stories by presenting introductory information with **the** as if it is old information and the narrative has already begun.

7 ***The boy** with fair hair lowered himself down the last few feet of rock and began to pick his way toward **the lake**.*

Associated and condensed information

We can express associated information with **the** and a different noun. In most cases, the connection is between two nouns, based on common knowledge (a house usually has a kitchen).

8 *We were thinking of buying **a house** in Victoria, but **the kitchen** was too small.*

9 *Luckily there was **a taxi** available and **the driver** knew how to get to the arena.*

10 *She's written **a** new **book**. I can't remember **the title**. **The cover** is red with gold letters.*

In some cases, the connection is between a verb and a noun.

11 *I really liked it, but didn't **buy** it because **the price** was too high.*

12 *He **asked** me about you. There was something odd about **the tone** of **the question**.*

13 *We were **driving** through heavy rain when **the windshield wipers** stopped working.*

14 *I **worked** there for a while, but **the pay** was terrible.*

We can also repeat information in a condensed way with **the** plus a compound noun. We can combine elements of information from one or more sentences to form the compound noun.

15 ***The curve** that indicates **supply** can **shift** in response to many factors that can't be measured. However, **the supply curve shift** can be measured.*

16 *You have to fill out a **form** to **apply** for a **credit card**. **The credit card application form** actually represents a contract.*

A Add these nouns, plus *a / an* or *the*, to these sentences.

bicycle, board, movie, job, owner, pay, price, restaurant, store, teacher

1 Suzy got .... part-time .... in ....
   Italian ...., but .... was really low.

2 I found .... old .... in a small store.
   .... said it had been his son's.

3 In class, ... always writes things on ....

4 According to Canuck Cinemas, it will cost you more to see ....
   this summer. .... increase will take effect on June 1st.

B Write appropriate articles (*a*, *the*, or no article (Ø)) in this introduction to a short story.

Inside (▶) ..the... station café it was warm and light. (1) .... wood of (2) .... tables shone from wiping and there were (3) .... baskets of (4) .... pretzels in glazed paper sacks. (5) .... chairs were carved, but (6) .... seats were worn and comfortable. There was (7) .... carved wooden clock on (8) .... wall and (9) .... bar at (10) .... far end of (11) .... room. Outside (12) .... window it was snowing.

C Choose an ending (a–j) for each beginning (1–10) and add *a*, *one*, *the*, or no article (Ø).

1 There was .... dog wandering outside (...)
2 She's spending .... July in the hospital. (...)
3 I can't understand .... finance report (...)
4 There was only .... toilet paper roll left (...)
5 There's .... girl pounding on the grand piano. (...)
6 We're going to buy .... new lawnmower. (...)
7 .... young boy had gone missing. (...)
8 She has .... terrible cough. (...)
9 He spent his teenage years indoors, worrying about .... pimples. (...)
10 As I told you, ... my computer keeps crashing. (...)

a She's really banging the instrument.
b Youth is really wasted on the young!
c The police needed people to help with the search.
d so Ariana stopped to help .... poor animal.
e I'll get rid of it and get .... new one.
f because the language is too technical.
g so the stuff was treated like .... gold.
h The old one was always breaking down.
i The problem won't go away without .... medical treatment.
j It isn't .... happiest time of her life, I'm sure.

D The following parts of a description of a car accident are not in the correct order. Write the numbers in the best order to describe how the accident happened.

4 .-...-...-...-...-...-...

1 There was a van behind the tour bus.
2 I saw a tour bus coming down the street towards me.
3 The bus signalled that it was turning right onto the side street,
4 ~~When I was waiting to cross Centre Street,~~
5 There was also a small car waiting to pull out from a side street and turn left.
6 but it couldn't complete the turn because of the car.
7 and it crashed right into the car.
8 But the van had already started to pass the bus
9 So the car started to pull out and turn left.

All and both, half and whole, each and every, either and neither

All and both

We use **all** before plural nouns and uncountable nouns to make very general statements (1) and **all (of)** before determiners plus nouns to make more specific statements (2).

1 *All cars have brakes.* • *All students must wear uniforms.* • *All information is confidential.*
2 *All (of) these cars are for sale.* • *All (of) the information you asked for is on our website.*

We use **all of** (not **all**) before pronouns (3). We use **everyone/everything** rather than **all** by itself (4).

3 *Did you write down their phone numbers? ~ No, not **all of them.*** (NOT *all them*)
4 *Everyone laughed at his jokes.* • *Everything was a mess.* (NOT *All was a mess.*)

We use **both** instead of **all** and **both of** instead of **all of** when we talk about two things or people.

5 *Use **both** hands to hold it.* • ***Both (of)** my brothers are older than me.* • ***Both of** them live in St. John's.*

We can use **all** and **both** for emphasis after subjects and pronoun objects (6) or after auxiliary verbs and **be** (7).

6 *The men **all** agreed to wait.* • *Juan explained it **all.*** • *We **both** need a vacation.* • *I like them **both.***
7 *We had **all** heard about the two Williams sisters. They were **both** very talented.*

Half and whole

We use **half** before determiners (8) or between determiners and nouns (9) to talk about measured amounts. We sometimes use **half (of)** when we are talking about approximately half (10).

8 *A pint is more than **half** a litre.* • *We'll be there in **half** an hour.* (NOT *half of an hour*)
9 *Get a **half** litre if you can.* • *A **half** hour should be long enough.* (NOT *a half of hour*)
10 *I've only answered **half (of)** the questions.* • *I lost **half (of)** my money.* • *Take **half (of)** this pie.*
We use **half of** before pronouns: *I can't eat **half of** it.* (NOT *I can't eat half it.*)

We use **whole** between a determiner and a singular noun (11) and **the whole of** before determiners, pronouns, and proper nouns for places (12) to emphasize a full or complete amount.

11 *The **whole** area had changed.* • *I can't eat a **whole** pie!* • *The woman told us her **whole** life story.*
12 *I spent **the whole of** this past weekend in bed.* • *The strike is affecting **the whole of** Quebec.*

A Choose an answer (a–d) for each question (1–4) and add *all, both, half,* or *whole*.

1 How much longer will the rain last? (...)   a You can have .... of them for $5.
2 How much is 16 ounces? (...)   b It might go on like this for the .... week.
3 How much are those two books? (...)   c .... of it, so he's penniless now.
4 How much money did he lose? (...)   d I think it's almost .... a kilogram.

B Write one of these quantifiers in each space. Add *of* where necessary.

all (×2), both (×2), half, no, none, one (×2), whole

Nowadays, (1) .... young girls can play football if they want to. When I was young, I really wanted to play football, but (2) .... girls were allowed to in my school. In fact, (3) .... the girls was allowed to play any "boys' sports." It was just (4) .... the rules. I learned about the game from my father and my uncle. (5) .... them had been football players and they often watched games on TV. I knew that (6) .... teams in a game had 11 players on the field and (7) .... them had special positions. I learned that there was a break after 15 minutes, then half-time, when (8) .... the game was over, a break after another 15 minutes, and that when 60 minutes had passed the (9) .... game was finished. It was fun to watch, but I would rather have been (10) .... the players.

Each and every

We use **each** and **every** before singular countable nouns. We use **each** when we're talking about two or more people or things separately (13). We use **every** when we're talking about three or more people or things together (14).

    13 *Each day is better than the last.* • *He came in with a cup in each hand.* (NOT … ~~in every hand.~~)
    14 *Every window was broken.* • *The Fogals go to Halifax every year.* (NOT … ~~every years.~~)

We use **each of** (not **every of**) before determiners with plural nouns (15) and plural pronouns (16). We can put **each** (not **every**) in different positions (17).

    15 *Each of her toenails was a different colour.* (NOT ~~Each her toenails~~ …)
    16 *Each of you must work alone.* • *Give a pen to each of them.* (NOT … ~~every (of) them.~~)
    17 *We each got one piece.* • *We were each given one piece.* • *We were given one piece each.*

We use **every** (not **each**) when we want to emphasize "as many / much as possible" (18), when we describe something happening at regular intervals (19), and after **almost** and **nearly** (20).

    18 *He had every opportunity to complete the work.* • *We wish you every success in your new job.*
    19 *There's a bus every 10 minutes.* • *Take two tablets every four hours.* (NOT … ~~each four hours.~~)
    20 *His team lost almost every game.* • *We run nearly every day.* (NOT ~~We run nearly each day.~~)

Either and neither

We use **either** before singular nouns (21) and **either of** before determiners plus plural nouns or pronouns (22) to indicate "one or the other" of two people or things.

    21 *Either parent can sign the form.* • *Left or right? ~ You can go either way.* (NOT … ~~either ways.~~)
    22 *Either of the parents can sign.* • *Coke or Pepsi? ~ I'd be happy with either of them, thanks.*

We use **neither / neither of** instead of **either / either of** when we mean "not one and not the other" of two people or things. We use singular verbs after subjects beginning with **neither of** in formal situations.

    23 *Neither parent has signed it.* • *Neither of the boxes was big enough.* • *Neither of us likes coffee.*

C Using a dictionary if necessary, complete the sentences with these words.

choice, doubles, either, neither (×2), quarterly, couple, each (×2), every, pair, twins

1 Behind the teacher came four young boys, dressed in grey uniforms, walking in pairs,
    .... holding hands.
2 Jeff Gulley and Ian McRoberts were actually .... who had been adopted by
    different families when they were born and .... of them knew about the other
    until they were almost 40 years old.
3 The .... was between a boat trip or a bus tour around the island and
    .... would have been fine with me, but Fatima wasn't feeling well and didn't
    want to leave the hotel.
4 Randy and Tracy are a young .... who have been together for about three years,
    but .... of them wants to get married.
5 Next year you'll have to send $400 in .... payments, which is $100
    .... three months.
6 In a mixed .... match in tennis, ... team consists of a man and
    a woman.

Many, much, and a lot (of); more and most

Many, much, and a lot (of)

When we talk about large numbers and amounts in a vague way, we can use **many** before plural nouns (1), **much** before uncountable nouns (2), and **a lot of** before both types of nouns (3).
1 ***Many*** *people believe in life after death.* • *There are **many** ways to improve your health.*
2 *How **much** money did you bring?* • *Please hurry, because there isn't **much** time left.*
3 *I used to eat **a lot of** doughnuts when I studied. I drank **a lot of** coffee too.* (NOT ~~a lot coffee~~)

We usually use **many / much** in formal situations and **a lot of** or **lots of** in informal situations. When we refer to a large number or amount in a specific way, we use **many of** before determiners plus plural nouns or plural pronouns (4) and **much of** before determiners plus uncountable nouns or singular pronouns (5). We can use **much of** (not **many of**) with singular countable nouns or proper nouns for places when we mean "a large part of" (6).
4 ***Many of*** *their customers have complained. **Many of** them have started going to other stores.*
5 *How **much of** your time is devoted to research? ~ Not **much of** it, I'm afraid.*
6 *Cats spend **much of** the day asleep.* • *It will be a dry sunny day over **much of** Newfoundland.*

We can use **many** and **much** without nouns.
7 *People still use butter in cooking, but **many** say they don't use as **much** as before.*
We can also use **a lot** (not **a lot of**) without a noun in informal situations: *We don't need a lot.*

We usually use **many** and **much** in questions and negatives (8). We can use them in positive statements after **as, so,** and **too** (9). We can also use the phrases **a good / great deal** (**of**) instead of **much** (**of**), and **a large number** (**of**) instead of **many** (**of**), in positive statements, usually in formal situations (10).
8 *How **many** do you want?* • *How **much** do they cost?* • *There aren't **many** left.* • *I don't have **much** cash.*
9 *Take **as much** time as you need.* • *I have **so much** work to do!* • *You bought **too many** things.*
10 *It requires **a great deal of** money and **a large number of** dedicated people to run a school.*

We can use **many** (not **much**) after determiners (11) or before **a / an** (12) in formal situations.
11 *I'm just one of **her many** admirers.* • *He explained **the many** rules and regulations they had.*
12 *He had spent **many an** uncomfortable night in cheap hotel rooms with thin walls.*

We can use **much** (not **many**) as an adverb after negative verbs or before comparatives.
13 *I didn't sleep **much** last night because I was so worried.* • *I'm feeling **much** better now.*
We can use **a lot** as an adverb after positive and negative verbs: *The area had changed a lot.*

More and most

We use **more** and **most** instead of **much / many** in comparisons. We use **more** for "a larger number or amount" (14) and **most** for "the largest number or amount" (15).
14 ***More*** *children are being educated at home recently. They are spending **more** time with their parents.*
15 ***Most*** *teenagers say they have the **most** fun when they are shopping at the mall.*
We also use **more** and **most** before adjectives or adverbs: **more quickly, the most expensive.**

We can use **more of** and **most of** before determiners (16), pronouns (17), and proper nouns (18).
16 *I've already eaten **more of** the cake than I should.* • ***Most of*** *those bananas were rotten.*
17 *I really liked it, but I can't eat any **more of** it.* • *I had to throw **most of** them away.*
18 *I hope to see **more of** British Columbia during my next trip.* • ***Most of*** *Venice is under water.*

We can use other quantifiers before **more** (not **most**) with the meaning "additional."
19 *I don't need **much more** time, just **two more** hours.* • *Is there **any more** coffee?* • *There's **no more**.*

A Rewrite each sentence, adding *many* or *much*. Make any other necessary changes.

▶ There wasn't food left, but we weren't very hungry so we didn't need.

   There wasn't much food left, but we weren't very hungry so we didn't need much.

1 There hasn't been discussion of the new road, but older town residents are against it.

....

2 Did you ask how these postcards cost? How them are you going to buy?

....

3 I'll be later today because I have so different places to go to and there's so traffic in town.

....

4 I asked my classmates if they did homework and said they didn't do unless there was a test.

....

B Add *many*, *many of*, *much*, or *much of* to each of these sentences from an article on Canadians and hockey.

1 Hockey is important in the social lives of .... Canadians.
2 .... local arenas are the centre of activity in the early morning when young children practise with their hockey teams.
3 For .... the year, hockey fans of all ages follow their heroes in the NHL.
4 .... the larger Canadian cities have NHL teams, which always draw huge crowds.
5 .... Canadians, however, aren't hockey fans and don't have .... interest in watching or playing the sport.
6 Instead, ... these people prefer baseball, basketball, or football.

C Choose an ending (a–f) for each beginning (1–6) and add *more*, *more of*, *most*, or *most of*.

1 Saudi Arabia is very hot (...)   a so I have .... to spend.
2 I liked those pens so much (...)   b I am not very good at making speeches.
3 I earn a lot .... than you (...)   c but I don't like .... vegetables.
4 I can eat .... types of fruit, (...)   d and .... it is desert.
5 As .... you know, (...)   e but I can't eat any .... it.
6 The pie is really good, (...)   f that I bought two .... them.

D Complete this weather forecast with *many* (x2), *more* (x3), and *much* (x2).

There's not (1) .... sunshine in the forecast for this weekend and (2) .... areas will see (3) .... rain than usual for this time of the year. Saturday will start with some bright spells and scattered showers, (4) .... of them heavy, giving way to (5) .... persistent rain later in the afternoon. Southwest winds will bring (6) .... unsettled weather and rain to (7) .... of central Nova Scotia on Sunday.

(A) few and (a) little, fewer/fewest and less/least, and other quantifiers

A few and a little

When we refer to small numbers and amounts in a vague way, we can use **a few** before plural nouns (1) and **a little** before uncountable nouns (2). We can also use **a few** and **a little** without nouns (3).

1 *There may be **a few** minutes left at the end.* • *I brought **a few** pieces of paper.*
2 *There may be **a little** time left at the end.* • *If you add **a little** salt, the soup will taste better.*
3 *Do you want milk? ~ Just **a little**.* • *Did you see any stars? ~ There were **a few**.*
  (NOT ~~There was a few.~~)

When we refer to a small number or amount in a specific way, we use **a few of** before determiners or plural pronouns (4) and **a little of** before determiners or singular pronouns (5).

4 *I've seen **a few of** those cartoons that David Boswell draws. Janette has **a few of** them on her wall.*
5 *I use **a little of** this moisturizing cream when my skin feels dry. You only need **a little of** it.*

We can use **a little** as an adverb after verbs or before participle adjectives and comparatives.

6 *I only slept **a little**.* • *We were **a little** annoyed at first.* • *My mother is feeling **a little** better now.*

Few and little

We use **few** (not **a few**) and **little** (not **a little**) when we are referring to "not many or much," usually in formal situations (7). We often use **not (very) many** (instead of **few**) and **not (very) much** (instead of **little**) to emphasize a negative view of the quantity (8).

7 *The refugees have **few** possessions and **little** hope of returning home soon.* (NOT ~~a little hope~~)
8 *They don't have (very) **many** possessions. They don't have (very) **much** hope.*

We also use **few** and **little** between determiners and nouns when we want to emphasize that the small quantity is the complete number or amount, usually in formal situations.

9 *I quickly packed **my few** belongings and spent **the little** money I had on a one-way ticket home.*

Fewer/fewest and less/least

We use **fewer** and **less** instead of **few**/**little** in comparisons. We use **fewer** (for "a smaller number of") before plural nouns and **less** (for "a smaller amount of") before uncountable nouns.

10 *I've been trying to eat **fewer** snacks and **less** junk food as part of my diet.*

We can use **fewer of** and **less of** before determiners (11) and pronouns (12).

11 *There are **fewer of** those small stores now.* • *I'd like to spend **less of my** time in meetings.*
12 *The swans are back, but there are **fewer of them** this year.* • *Sugar isn't good for you. Eat **less of it**!*

We use **the fewest** (13) and **the least** (14) when we refer to the smallest number or amount.

13 *Ali made **the fewest** mistakes. Nick is the most cheerful and seems to have **the fewest** worries.*
14 *You complain that you make **the least** money here, but that's because you do **the least** work.*
We also use **least** and **less** before adjectives or adverbs: **less quickly**, **the least expensive**.

A **Choose an ending (a–e) for each beginning (1–5) and add** *a few, few, a little,* **or** *little,* **plus** *of* **where necessary.**

1 We had very .... problems living here (...)   a and the .... water that was left.
2 The teacher seemed .... disappointed (...)   b so I only ate .... it.
3 The homemade soup was very salty (...)   c and we've had .... sunny days too.
4 We shared the .... pieces of fruit (...)   d until our car was stolen .... days ago.
5 It's been .... warmer recently (...)   e that only .... us had done the work.

Multipliers

Multipliers are words and phrases such as **once**, **twice**, or **three times** that we use before determiners when we are talking about how often something happens (15) or how much more something is (16). We can also use multipliers plus **as ... as** with **many** or **much**, adjectives, and adverbs (17).

15 *I play hockey **once a** week.* • *I see my sister about **four times a** year.* • *We eat **three times a** day.*
16 *He sold it for **twice the** original price.* • *Those tomatoes are **two or three times the** average size.*
17 *We have **twice as many** knives **as** forks left.* • *She's paid **three times as much as** I am.* • *He can run **twice as fast as** I can.* • *Some of the essays were **twice as long as** mine.*

Fractions and percentages

We can use fractions (**a quarter, two-thirds**) with **of** before determiners and pronouns.

18 *It takes **a quarter of** an hour.* • *I only used **two-thirds of** the oil, so there's **a third of** it left.*

We can use **half** without **of** before determiners: *Half (of) my answers were wrong.*

We use percentages (**5%, five percent**) before nouns, or with **of** before determiners and pronouns.

19 *There was a **10%** increase.* • *They take **30 percent** of my pay. I get **70 percent** of it.*

Fractions and percentages with singular or uncountable nouns have singular verbs. With plural nouns, they have plural verbs.

20 ***Two-thirds** of the report **is** written.* • *About **20 percent** of the students **are** Asian.*

B **Using a dictionary if necessary, complete the sentences with these words and phrases. Add *of*, *as*, *a*, and *the* where necessary.**

~~eighth,~~ four times, once, quarter, twenty percent, twice, two-fifths

▶ A furlong is ...... an eighth of a ...... mile.
1 The money was divided equally among the four brothers, so each received
   .... it.
2 .... year we have our annual family gathering at my grandparents' house.
3 A centimetre is about .... an inch, or 0.394 inches to be exact.
4 A litre bottle holds almost .... much as a pint.
5 Did you know that at least .... ticket price goes toward taxes?
6 At $780,000, the selling price is almost .... price ($200,000) that Dan and
   Ginny Chauvin paid for their house just six years ago.

C **Add these words and phrases to the text.**

a few, fewer, fewest, fifty percent, little

Although the world's population is still increasing, the rate of growth has slowed down from 2.2 percent per year 50 years ago to about 1.1 percent per year today. There is (1) ....
chance that population growth will level off before 2050, but there are (2) ....
indications that the growth rate will probably keep declining. Women in the wealthiest countries continue to have the (3) .... children. However, partly because of better education and employment opportunities, many women in poorer countries are choosing to have (4) .... babies. In some places, the birth rate is now (5) ....
lower than just 30 years ago.

Reflexive and reciprocal pronouns

Reflexive pronouns: **myself, themselves**, etc.

The reflexive pronouns, or reflexives, are **myself, yourself, himself, herself, itself, ourselves, yourselves**, and **themselves**. We use a reflexive pronoun instead of an object pronoun when the object is the same person or thing as the subject.

    1 *Be careful or **you'll** hurt **yourself**. • I'm afraid **I** might cut **myself**.* (NOT ~~I'm afraid I might cut me.~~)
       • *Isn't it amazing how **the human body** heals **itself** after an injury?* (NOT … ~~the body heals it~~ …)
Reflexives have no possessive form. We use **my own**, etc. before nouns: *He has **his own** ideas.*

We can also use reflexives after most prepositions when the object of the preposition is the same as the subject (2). We use object pronouns (not reflexives) after prepositions of place such as **above, below, beside**, and **near** and verbs such as **bring** and **take** plus **with** (3).

    2 *Aliya never buys anything **for herself**. • Carlos only thinks **about himself**.*
    3 *Amy put the bag down **beside her**. • You should take an umbrella **with you**.* (NOT … ~~with yourself.~~)

We can also use reflexives for emphasis. We can use them after noun phrases and pronouns to emphasize a particular person or thing (4) or after verb phrases to emphasize "without help" (5).

    4 *This book was signed by the writer **herself**! • You **yourself** said that she was a great writer.*
    5 *I changed the flat tire **myself**. • Terrance and Marnie painted the whole house **themselves**.*
We use reflexives after **by** to emphasize "alone": *She lives by herself. • I'll do it by myself.*

There are some actions such as **shave** and **shower** that we usually describe without reflexives (6), but that we can describe with reflexives for special emphasis if, for example, the action is difficult (7).

    6 *Their father used to get up, shave, shower, get dressed, and make breakfast for all of them.*
    7 *But since his accident, he can't shave **himself** or even dress **himself** without their help.*

A **Choose an ending (a–d) for each beginning (1–4) and add appropriate pronouns.**

1 He got a hammer and some nails (…)	a and take care of ……………… .
2 Remember to eat well, exercise regularly, (…)	b and they saw the city below ……………… .
3 Thanks for offering to help, (…)	c and repaired it ……………… .
4 The plane started to descend (…)	d but I can do it ……………… .

Reciprocal pronouns: **each other** and **one another**

We can use the reciprocal pronouns **each other** and **one another** with no difference in meaning.

    8 *The cat and the dog hate **each other/one another**. • They always avoid **one another/each other**.*

We use reciprocal pronouns (9) instead of reflexives (10) when the same action or feeling goes both ways between two or more people or things.

    9 *The candidates described **each other**.* (= Each one described the other one.)
  10 *The candidates described **themselves**.* (= Each one described himself or herself.)

We can use reciprocal pronouns after prepositions (11) and as possessives (12).

  11 *The two girls never argued **with one other**. They were always chatting **to each other**.*
  12 *They even wore **each other's/one another's** clothes sometimes.*

We can use **each** as subject and **the other(s)** as object when the action of the verb goes both ways (13). When the action goes one way, we use **one** as subject and **the other(s)** as object (14).

  13 *I asked the boys if they had broken the window and **each** blamed **the other**.*
  14 *There are two buses at 5:30 and **one** always follows **the other** in case the first one gets full.*

B Add the pronouns *it, they, we,* and *you* plus appropriate reflexives to this text.

They say that if you want something done right, (1) .... have to do it
(2) .... And we all know that if something is broken, (3) .... certainly
won't fix (4) .... As a result, there are many more DIY ("Do It Yourself") stores in
Canada these days. It seems that (5) .... have all suddenly decided to do our home
repairs (6) .... So, are all the real contractors and plumbers out of work now?
Apparently not. They're even busier now, trying to fix the mess left by those who discovered that
(7) .... really couldn't do it (8) .... and had to call for professional help.

C Complete these sentences with the prepositions *about, by, for, near,* and *with,* plus appropriate pronouns.

1 Erica York was a self-taught mathematician who liked to spend hours
.... in the library.
2 The man seemed very self-centred and only wanted to talk ....
3 People who are self-employed work ...., not a company.
4 I took a small knife ...., hoping I would only have to use it in self-defence.
5 Test your self-restraint by placing something you really like to eat ....,
but don't eat it.

D Using a dictionary if necessary, complete these descriptions with one set of words (not necessarily in this order).

another / each / one / the other
another's / each / one / other's
each / other / you / yourself

1 Mutual respect is a feeling of admiration that people have for (1) ....
(2) .... equally, and self-respect is a feeling of pride in (3) .... and
the belief that what (4) .... do or say is right and good.
2 An exchange is an arrangement through which two people or groups from different countries
visit (5) .... (6) .... homes or do (7) ....
(8) .... jobs for a short time.
3 Wrestling is a sport in which two people fight by holding onto (9) ....
(10) .... while (11) .... tries to throw or force (12) ....
to the ground.

E Complete the sentences with appropriate forms of these verbs plus reflexive or reciprocal pronouns.

agree with, blame, express, hurt, meet

1 All students are required to give a presentation on their projects and to
.... as clearly as possible.
2 The boy said that his sister had slipped on the wet floor and ....
3 Both drivers said it wasn't their fault. They .... for the accident.
4 My aunt and uncle always seem to have different opinions about things and they almost never
....
5 Before they got married, Pankaj and Achara visited his parents in India and then her parents in
Thailand, so they could .... families.

Empty subjects **it** and **there**

Empty subject **it**

We use **it** as an empty subject with the verb **be** in expressions of time, distance, and weather.
  1 *It's 11 o'clock.* • *It's two kilometres to town.* • *Is **it** raining?* (NOT ~~Is raining?~~)

We use **it** + **be** before an adjective or noun plus a noun clause.
  2 *It's sad <u>that she's leaving so soon</u>.* • *It was just a coincidence <u>that we were both in London</u>.*

We can also use **it** + **be** before an adjective or noun plus a gerund (3) or infinitive (4).
  3 *It was nice <u>talking to you</u>.* • *It's an advantage <u>having a rich family</u>.*
  4 *It's not wise <u>to hike in the mountains by yourself</u>.* • *It might be an exaggeration <u>to say he's rich</u>.*

We can use a noun clause (5), gerund (6), or infinitive (7) as subject instead of **it** in formal situations.
We don't use a noun clause, infinitive, or gerund instead of **there** (8).
  5 *It was obvious <u>that Brazil was going to win</u>.* → *That Brazil was going to win was obvious.*
  6 *It's often a problem for Henrik <u>being so tall</u>.* → *Being so tall is often a problem for Henrik.*
  7 *It's a real pleasure <u>to meet you at last</u>.* → *To meet you at last is a real pleasure.*
  8 *There will be someone to meet you at the airport.* (NOT ~~To meet you at the airport will be someone.~~)

After **it** we usually use a form of the verb **be**, but we can use verbs such as **surprise** and **scare** plus
an object to describe a reaction (9) and verbs such as **seem** and **appear** to express a conclusion (10).
  9 *It **surprised** everyone that Marion won.* • *It really **scared** me to see the horse and rider fall.*
  10 *It **seems** that he was unhappy in Toronto.* • *It **appears** that he has been neglecting his studies.*

We can also use **it** as an empty object after "liking" (or "not liking") verbs before a noun clause (11)
and after verbs such as **find**, **make**, and **think** before an adjective plus a clause or infinitive (12).
After some verbs such as **regard**, **see**, and **view** used to express an opinion, we put **as** after **it** (13).
  11 *I **hate it** when the alarm suddenly goes off.* • *My parents **love it** that we live closer now.*
  12 *I **find it** surprising that you waited so long.* • *The loud music **made it** difficult to talk.* •
     *We **thought it** strange that he was still in his pyjamas.* (NOT ~~We thought strange that he was~~ ...)
  13 *They **regard it as** encouraging that both sides are willing to continue negotiations.*

A Rewrite these sentences in a less formal style beginning with *it*.

  1 That Toni never helps with the cleaning really annoys everyone.

  ....

  2 Not having a car can be a big disadvantage.

  ....

  3 To see potential problems in advance is very important in my job.

  ....

  4 Why she left so suddenly was a complete mystery.

  ....

  5 To discover that your passport was missing must have been a shock.

  ....

  6 That people can eat such unhealthy food and live so long always amazes me.

  ....

Empty subject **there**

We use **there** as an empty subject with the verb **be** before a noun phrase. The noun phrase determines whether the verb is singular or plural. We often include an adverbial, such as a preposition phrase of place (**in** *Travel* **magazine**) or time (**on Friday**) after the noun phrase.

    14 ***There was*** *an article in* Travel *magazine about Munich.* • ***There are*** *two meetings on Friday.*
In informal situations, **there's** is often used with plural nouns: *Don't forget there's two meetings.*

We use **there** + **be** to say (15) or ask if (16) people and things are present or exist (or not).

    15 ***There was*** *an old man in the waiting room.* • ***There are*** *no snakes in Ireland.*
    16 ***Are there*** *any questions?* • ***Is there*** *a bathroom upstairs?* (NOT ~~Is a bathroom upstairs?~~)
We don't use **it** to say or ask if things are present or exist. (NOT ~~Is it a bathroom upstairs?~~)

We can use **there** (not **it**) + **be** with quantifiers to present information about amounts and quantities.

    17 ***There's*** *a lot of crime now in the city centre.* • ***There wasn't*** *much room inside his car.*
        (NOT ~~A lot of crime is now in the city centre.~~ • ~~It wasn't much room inside his car.~~)

When we express an opinion about things being present or existing, we can put modals and / or adverbs such as **certainly** or **probably** between **there** and **be** (18). We can also put **seem** or **appear** between **there** and **to be** (19).

    18 ***There should be*** *a guard rail here.* • ***There certainly are*** *problems.* • ***There will probably be*** *a fight.*
    19 ***There seem to be*** *a lot of unanswered questions.* • ***There didn't appear to be*** *anyone in charge.*

We can also use **there** + **be** with adjectives such as **likely** and **sure** plus **to be** and a noun phrase to show how certain we are about the information being reported.

    20 ***There isn't likely to be*** *peace for many years.* • ***There are sure to be*** *protests about the decision.*

We can use the passive forms of verbs such as **report**, **say**, and **think** between **there** and **to be** to report information, but we don't usually use a passive after **there**.

    21 ***There were thought to be*** *some problems in the original design and indeed a number of flaws were found.* (NOT *...* ~~and indeed there were found a number of flaws.~~)

After **there** + **be**, we usually introduce new information with **a / an** or indefinite pronouns (22), but we can use **the** or demonstratives when we treat information as familiar or given (23).

    22 ***Is there*** *a problem?* ~ *Yes, I think* ***there's something*** *wrong because* ***there's a long lineup***.
    23 *I think we should go early.* ***There's the problem*** *of parking and when we go later* ***there's*** *always* ***that long lineup*** *to get into the parking lot.*

A **Correct the mistakes in the use of *there* and *it* in these sentences.**

              there
  ▶ I'm sure ~~it~~ will be someone to help you with your luggage.

1 It was such a nice day in the valley that it was a surprise to hear there was snowing in the mountains.

2 It isn't much time left to prepare for the meeting if it's first thing tomorrow morning.

3 There certain to be questions about Confederation on the history test.

4 It was said to be hundreds of people stranded by the floods.

5 A lot of fat and sugar is in pies and cakes.

6 Everyone found very amusing that I'd started taking karate lessons.

7 They viewed it offensive that he just slumped in the chair and put his feet up on the coffee table.

8 It really wasn't surprising that there were found no survivors in the wreckage of the plane.

Substitution

One and ones

Substitution is the use of forms such as **one**, **ones**, **so**, and **do so** instead of noun phrases, verb phrases, and clauses. (*"Is it a real **one**?" asked Eddie. "I think **so**," said Ava.*)

We can use **one** and **ones** instead of repeating countable nouns (1). We use **one** instead of a singular noun (**peach**) or a noun phrase (**a small ripe peach**) (2). We use **ones** instead of a plural noun (**peaches**), but not instead of a plural noun phrase (**these small peaches**) (3).

    1 *We bought peaches at the farmers' market. Would you like **one**? ~ Oh, I love the small **ones**.*
    2 *I'm not sure if there's a small **one** that's ripe. ~ Oh, yes, there's **one** here.*
    3 *I've never seen these small **ones** in the grocery store.* (NOT *~~I've never seen ones~~...*)

Instead of repeating plural noun phrases (4) or uncountable nouns (5), we use **some** or **any**.

    4 *I love these small peaches, but I've never seen **any** in the grocery store. I must get **some**.*
    5 *I'm going to buy more fruit. Do you need **any**? I'll get **some** for the picnic.* (NOT *~~some ones~~*)

We use **one** to talk about an object in general (6) and **it** for a specific example of an object (7).

    6 *Do you have a French dictionary? I'm looking for **one**.* (= not a specific French dictionary)
    7 *Do you have the French dictionary? I'm looking for **it**.* (= a specific French dictionary)

We don't usually use **a/an** with **one** (8) or quantifiers with **ones** (9) unless we include an adjective.

    8 *I need a pen, preferably **a red one**. Do you have **one**?* (NOT *~~Do you have a one?~~*)
    9 *Most of the tomatoes were still green, but I picked out **three ripe ones**.* (NOT *~~three ones~~*)
We can use **each/every** with **one**: *I examined each/every one.*

We don't usually use **the** with **one** or **ones** unless there is an adjective before them (10), or a descriptive phrase or clause after them (11).

    10 *We bought a new table, so you can have **the old one**.* (NOT *... ~~you can have the one.~~*)
    11 *Do you mean **the one in the kitchen** or **the one that used to have the computer on it**?*

We usually use demonstrative pronouns or possessive pronouns (rather than determiners with **one** or **ones**) (12) unless we include an adjective (13).

    12 *I put our books in two piles. **These** are **mine** and **those** are **yours**.* (NOT *... ~~those ones are your ones.~~*)
    13 *Computers have changed a lot. **My new one** is so much faster than **that other one** I used to have.*
In informal situations, **that one**, **this one**, etc. are sometimes used.

A **Choose an ending (a–d) for each beginning (1–4) and add these words.**

any, it, one, ones (×2), some, them

1 Sharon: I need six large brown envelopes. (...)	a but .... wasn't large enough.
2 Radha: We have a lot of small ...., (...)	b but he may have used .... already.
3 Ask Jacques, he had .... earlier, (...)	c but no large ...., I'm afraid.
4 Sharon: I got .... from him, (...)	d Do you have ....?

B **Correct the mistakes in this text.**

My grandmother told me this story about her first fridge. After my parents got married, they rented an apartment. She said it was a very small_ʌ with an oven, but no fridge, so they started looking for it in the newspaper. She said that fridges weren't as common then and some ones were really expensive. But she kept looking for it. She eventually found a second-hand that wasn't too expensive and the man said he would deliver it for free, so she bought right away. She was really happy. She waited a week, then two weeks, but she never saw the man or the fridge again. Later, she heard about some other people who had gone to see that man and his fridge and every had fallen for the same trick.

So and do so

We can use **so** instead of repeating a clause after some verbs expressing opinions or expectations.

14 *The rain will stop soon. ~ I hope* **so.** (= I hope the rain will stop soon.) (NOT *I hope it.*)

Other verbs used in this way include **be afraid, believe, expect, guess, think**

We don't use **so** after **be sure** and **know**: *It's getting late. ~ I know.* (NOT *I know so.*)

To express the negative, we use **so** after the negative forms of **believe, expect,** and **think** (15).
We use **not** after the positive forms of **be afraid, guess,** and **hope** (16).

15 *Perhaps it will be nice and sunny. ~ I don't think* **so.** (NOT *I don't think. / I don't think it.*)

16 *The weather may actually get worse. ~ I hope* **not.** (NOT *I don't hope so. / I don't hope it.*)

We also use **so** after **say** and **tell** (someone) instead of repeating what was said.

17 *Jones was fired. They said* **so** *on the news.* (= They said that Jones was fired on the news.)
I thought it was a mistake to fire him and I told them **so.** (NOT ... *I told them it.*)

We can use **if so** instead of repeating a clause in a conditional sentence.

18 *Linda says you took her book.* **If so,** *you must return it.* (= If you took her book, ...)

We can use **so** after **less** and **more** instead of repeating an adjective (19) or an adverb (20).

19 *He used to be really serious. He's* **less so** *now.* (= He's less serious now.)

20 *They're working hard, even* **more so** *than usual.* (= even harder than usual)

We can use different forms of **do** plus **so** instead of repeating the same verb and object.

21 *They asked me to revise the first paragraph and I* **did so.** (= I revised the first paragraph.) •
Anne Shirley refused Gilbert Blythe's offer of marriage, then regretted **doing so.**

We usually use **do so** in formal situations. In informal situations, we can use **do it** or **do that** (22).
When we repeat the verb with a different subject, we use **do it** (not **do so**) (23).

22 *Jump across the stream. Come on. Just* **do it!** *~ Oh, no. It's too far. I can't* **do that.**

23 *Brandon forgot to take the garbage out and I can't* **do it.** *Can you* **do it?** (NOT *Can you do so?*)

A **Complete these sentences with *so* or *it* plus appropriate forms of *do* where necessary.**

1 Adam likes to drive fast, even more .... since he got that new sports car.

2 Did we miss the bus? ~ I'm afraid .... Will there be another one? ~ I certainly
hope .... !

3 Can you complete the work today? ~ I don't think .... I'm sure I can't
.... before Friday.

4 WARNING. Dangerous currents. Anyone who swims here .... at their own risk.

5 One of my friends has asked me to go snowboarding, but I've never .... before.

6 Many teenagers want to earn money working part-time jobs and are encouraged
.... by their parents.

B **Complete this dialogue with *one, ones, so,* or Ø (= nothing).**

"Would you like to hear a joke? Have you heard the (1) .... about the five flies?"

    "I don't think (2) ...."

    "Okay. If there are five flies on the table and I kill one, how many will be left?"

    "I'm not sure (3) .... Will there be four (4) .... left?"

    "Wrong! There'll only be the dead (5) ...."

    "What about the other (6) .... ?"

    "Well, they'll fly away, of course!"

    "Ha! I should have known (7) ...."

Ellipsis

Ellipsis is the process of leaving out words and phrases instead of repeating them. (*Ava looked around quickly, then ___ reached down, ___ grabbed the money, and ___ hurried out of the room.*)

A Write the numbers of the appropriate examples in the spaces.

Leaving words out

Ellipsis means leaving words out. Instead of repeating a noun phrase (**the guard**), we can use a pronoun or we can leave the pronoun out ▢. Instead of repeating a verb phrase (**take**), we can use a substitution form or leave the substitution form out ▢.

1 *The guard looked over and <u>he</u> smiled. / The guard looked over and _ smiled.*
2 *She could take the money, but she won't <u>do it</u>. / She could take the money, but she won't _ _ .*

We usually use ellipsis instead of repeating words before nouns in phrases joined by **and**, **but**, or **or**.

3 *You'll need a pen **or** _ pencil. • Ashley's aunt **and** _ uncle own property in BC **and** _ Newfoundland.*
We can also use ellipsis after a comma in a list: *I'm afraid of bees, _ wasps, and _ spiders.*

Leaving out subjects and objects

After **and**, **but**, or **or** in compound sentences, we usually leave out a repeated subject ▢, a repeated subject and auxiliary ▢, or a repeated subject and verb ▢.

4 *She was shouting **and** _ _ throwing things. • Should we bring our bags **or** _ _ leave them here?*
5 *We sat **and** _ talked. • He came, **but** _ left early. • They ran **or** _ walked the rest of the way.*
6 *He looked okay, **but** _ _ tired. • I enjoy movies, _ _ going to the theatre, **and** _ _ walks in the park.*

We can also leave out repeated subjects in later clauses after **then** and **yet** ▢. We don't usually leave out subjects (and auxiliaries) after subordinating conjunctions ▢.

7 *We cleaned up **before** <u>we</u> left. • He's tired **because** <u>he's</u> sick. (NOT ~~He's tired because sick.~~)*
8 *The bird looked up, **then** _ suddenly flew away. • Ayo liked Canada, **yet** _ longed for Nigeria.*

We usually leave out repeated objects ▢ or prepositional phrases ▢ from the first clause. We use an object pronoun rather than leave out the object from second or later clauses ▢.

9 *We gave food _ _ and water to everyone. • I lived _ _ _ _ _ and studied in Rome for a year.*
10 *She makes _ and sells jewellery. • We usually boil _ _ or poach some eggs for breakfast.*
11 *She makes jewellery and sells it. (NOT ~~She makes jewellery and sells.~~)*

Leaving out verb phrases

After an auxiliary verb in the second or later clause, we usually leave out a repeated verb phrase ▢. We can leave out repeated adjectives and prepositional phrases after **be** as a linking verb ▢.

12 *We thought they would be late, but they **weren't** _. • I'm afraid he's in love and she **isn't** _ _ .*
13 *I've seen the movie, but Miguel **hasn't** _ _ _ . • The boys weren't feeling cold, but I **was** _ _ . •*
   *We would help you if we **could** _ _ . • Sara will eat broccoli, but Jaleesa **won't** _ _ .*

We can also leave out a repeated verb phrase after infinitive **to** ▢ or **not to** ▢. After verbs such as **agree** and **want**, we can also leave out **to** ▢.

14 *She'll leave unless he begs her not to _. • Some boys kept talking after I told them not to _.*
15 *I don't smoke now, but I used to _. • We haven't applied for a grant, but we plan to _ soon.*
16 *They asked us to do this and you agreed (to) _ _ . • You can stay here if you want (to) _.*
After a negative, we include **to**: *He'd like me to stay, but I don't want to. (NOT ... ~~but I don't want.~~)*

In formal situations, a repeated verb can be left out of a second clause when both clauses have the same structure ▢. We usually repeat the verb when the subject is a pronoun ▢.

17 *The girls go first and the boys _ after them. • Alex chose the University of Alberta and Alison _ Windsor.*
18 *We go first and they go after us. (NOT ~~We go first and they after us.~~)*

We can leave out repeated words after question words when we ask ▢ or report questions ▢.

19 *I have to leave now. ~ Why _? • It will cost a lot of money to repair the damage. ~ How much _?*
20 *Dr. Foster has said she's planning to go on vacation, but she hasn't told us where _ or when _ yet.*

B Complete the definitions using one of the following nouns plus *they*, *them*, or Ø (= nothing).

litter, pollution, trash, waste

(1) .... : small pieces of paper or containers that people leave, (2) ....
drop, or (3) .... throw away in a public place.
(4) .... : the act of using things in a careless way, causing (5) .... to be
lost or (6) .... destroyed (7) .... unnecessarily.
(8) .... : the substances that make air, water, or soil dirty and (9) ....
make (10) .... unsuitable for people to use.
(11) .... : things that people throw away because (12) .... no longer
want or (13) .... need (14) ....

C Choose the best ending for each beginning and write it in the space, leaving out appropriate words.

we are hoping to leave soon, she didn't want to come with us, he didn't help us move it,
we can go by train, she's working in Iqaluit, no one was caught, I sat in the back,
she wouldn't tell us what she found, the others hadn't been there

▶ We're packing our bags and *hoping to leave soon.* ....
1 We can go to Edmonton by bus or ....
2 Elizabeth is working in Inuvik or ....
3 I didn't think anyone would be caught and ....
4 Laila found something, but ....
5 We had already been to Athens, but ....
6 Callum could have helped us move the table, but ....
7 My grandparents sat in front and ....
8 I invited Malia to come with us, but ....

D Create the shortest possible version of this text by drawing a line through the repeated words that could be left out of each sentence.

He put the money on the table and ~~he~~ sat down. He sat in his hot clothes and he felt heavy. The woman looked over at him and she smiled. Her smile said she was in charge and she could take his money if she wanted to take his money. Of course she could take his money, he thought, but obviously she didn't want to take his money yet. The smile lingered for a moment or two longer, then it disappeared and it was replaced by a dark stare.

"I asked you to pay me a thousand and you agreed to pay me a thousand. This is only five hundred."

"You'll get your thousand. I'll give you half of your thousand now and I'll give you the other half of your thousand later when I get the orchid."

"I could get the orchid and I could find someone else who'd want to buy it."

"You won't find someone else who'd want to buy it. Nobody else is even looking for this orchid."

The dark stare wanted to stay, but it was slowly replaced by half a smile. It said she would give me half of the smile now and the other half of the smile later.

Participle adjectives, compound adjectives, and adjectives as nouns

Participle adjectives

We use adjectives derived from present participles (**surprising**) to describe the source or cause of an action or feeling (1). We use adjectives derived from past participles (**surprised**) to describe the one(s) affected by the action or feeling (2).

    1 *The news was **surprising**.* • *The teacher drew a very **confusing** diagram on the board.*
    2 *My parents were **surprised**.* • *The **confused** students said that they couldn't understand it.*

We can treat people and other living things as the source of a feeling (**He's boring**) or the ones affected by it (**I'm bored**) (3). We treat non-living things as the source only (**It's boring**) (4).

    3 *Darwin was a **fascinating** person.* • *I was **disappointed**.* • *Why is the dog getting so **excited**?*
    4 *Mars is a **fascinating** planet.* • *The news was **disappointing**.* (NOT *~~The news was disappointed.~~*)

A **Choose an ending (a–d) for each beginning (1–4) and add participle adjectives created from these verbs.**

astonish, exhaust, irritate, worry

1 I think it's very .... (...)
2 Ms. Pellarin seemed .... (...)
3 They were really .... (...)
4 The .... tricks of magicians (...)

a are revealed in a new book.
b after they had walked 10 kilometres.
c that she might not have enough money.
d when students come in late.

Compound adjectives

Compound adjectives can consist of an adjective, adverb, or noun and either a present participle or a past participle (5). Compounds with present participles are often based on active verbs (6). Compounds with past participles are often based on passive verbs (7).

    5 *I'm in **slow-moving** traffic.* • *Was it a **well-planned** trip?* (NOT *... ~~a planned-well trip?~~*)
    6 *Modern Maids is the name of a **house-cleaning** service.* (= a service which <u>cleans</u> houses)
    7 *I'd really like a **home-cooked** meal for a change.* (= a meal that <u>is cooked</u> at home)
Others include **energy-saving**, **life-threatening**, **low-paid**, **urgently needed**, **well-trained**

There are some compound adjectives that consist of combinations of adjectives and nouns (8) or adverbs and adjectives (9).

    8 *He likes **fast-food** restaurants.* • *Let's try to get **front-row** seats.* • *Do you have a **full-time** job?*
    9 *Separatism is a **highly sensitive** issue.* • *There are a lot of **politically independent** voters.*

Adjectives as nouns

We can use some adjectives after **the** as nouns to refer to specific groups of people in society. These noun phrases are plural, without -s.

    10 ***The young** aren't happier than **the elderly**.* • ***The disadvantaged** should be cared for by **the wealthy**.*
Note that we can also say **young people** or **a young person**. (NOT *~~the youngs~~* or *~~a young~~*)

We can also use **the** before adjectives describing nationality (**Italians, Cubans**) to talk about the people, their governments, their national teams, etc. These noun phrases are plural, but we don't add -s to words ending in -ch, -sh, -se, -ss.

    11 ***The Italians** are here and **the French** have also agreed to send a peacekeeping force.* •
    *The United Nations proposal has support from **the Canadians**, **the Japanese**, and **the Swiss**.*

We use some adjectives after **the** to refer to an abstract idea. These noun phrases are singular.

    12 ***The unknown** isn't the same as **the impossible**.* • *In sports, **the unpredictable** often happens.*

B Add these adjectives to the text.

amazed, amazing, annoyed, annoying, bored, boring, interested, interesting

Monday was a PA day and, unfortunately, it rained all day, so the children kept telling me they
were (1) .... and there was nothing (2) .... to do at home. I was trying
to write some of my reports, but they kept interrupting me every five minutes and just became
very (3) .... I'm (4) .... that their teachers can keep them busy and
(5) .... in their lessons every day. After only one morning with them, I was extremely
(6) .... because of the constant noise and arguing. I was ready to scream. Instead,
I decided to take them to the movies. It's really (7) .... to see how calm they can
become in a dark theatre. The movie seemed kind of (8) ...., but at least it kept
them quiet.

**C Make appropriate compound adjectives from each pair of words and add them to the
sentences.**

distance / long, end / never, ~~grow / fast~~, keep / peace, educate / well, funny / look,
home / make, wash / white

▶ Ghana had to increase food imports to meet the needs of a ... fast-growing ... population.
1 Ms. Amodeo offered us bread and her .... jam.
2 Please don't use this phone to make any .... calls.
3 Soldiers have to learn to talk rather than fight when they are sent on .... missions.
4 The prime minister's wife seemed to have a .... supply of new shoes and purses.
5 We have to invest more in schools and teachers if we want to have a .... population.
6 That .... piece of cloth at the end of each sleeve is called a frill.
7 We rented a small cottage in Muskoka, with a red roof and .... walls.

D Correct the mistakes in this text.

Sometimes I wonder what people in other countries think about us. We are no longer among the rich

and powerfuls of Europe. In a very short period, we seem to have turned into the poor and weaks.

The situation is appalled. You cannot walk down a street in our cities without seeing a homeless.

The unemployeds stand around on our street corners. The elderly and sick receives no help. Why

are we no longer shocking that this is going on? Is it like this everywhere? Does the Japanese and

the Canadian have the same problems? I doubt it. The unthinkable have happened here and we

must do something about it soon.

Adverbs of degree, manner, viewpoint, and comment

Degree adverbs

We use degree adverbs to say to what extent something is done or felt. We use some degree adverbs such as **really** or **completely** in mid position or end position in sentences.

   1 *He **totally** forgot.* • *She **really** hates fish.* • *We failed **completely**.* • *Prices increased **moderately**.*

We usually use some degree adverbs such as **pretty, quite,** or **very** before adjectives and adverbs (2). We can also use the phrases **a bit** and **a little** as degree adverbs before adjectives and adverbs (3), but we don't use them with adjectives before nouns.

   2 *They're **pretty** good.* • *It's **quite** tasty.* • *We listened **very** carefully.*

   3 *She's feeling **a little** tired.* • *The music is **a bit** loud.* (NOT *It's a bit loud music.*)

We don't use **very** before verbs: *I'm not enjoying it **very much**.* (NOT *I'm not very enjoying it.*)

We can use **more / less** and **most / least** as degree adverbs in comparatives and superlatives.

   4 *Going by train can be **more** convenient than flying in Europe and it's usually **less** expensive.*

We also use **too** before adjectives and adverbs and **enough** after them.

   5 *It's **too** difficult.* • *He spoke **too** quietly.* • *Is this box big **enough**?* • *You didn't leave early **enough**.*

Manner adverbs

We use manner adverbs to indicate how something is done. We usually put them in end position.

   6 *I'll read it **carefully**.* • *He writes **clearly**.* • *They searched the room **quickly** and **thoroughly**.*

Note that we put manner before time: *She works **hard** now.* (NOT *She works now hard.*)

Manner adverbs are sometimes used, especially in literature, to describe how something was said.

   7 *"I have a flashlight, just follow me," she said **nervously**.*

     *"I would follow you to the end of the world," he whispered **hoarsely** in reply.*

Others include **angrily, anxiously, cheerfully, gloomily, impatiently, passionately, seriously**

Viewpoint adverbs

We use viewpoint adverbs to describe the perspective or point of view being considered. We usually put them in end position (8), or in front position with a comma (9).

   8 *It did well **commercially**.* • *They're working **individually**.* • *It was not done **scientifically**.*

   9 ***Financially**, the project makes sense.* ***Psychologically** and **socially**, it's a terrible idea.*

Comment adverbs

We use comment adverbs to include a comment or opinion about what is being said or written. We can use some of them, such as **probably**, in mid position, but we usually put comment adverbs such as **surprisingly** or **of course** in front or end position with commas.

   10 *It was **probably** a misunderstanding.* • ***Surprisingly**, he failed.* • *I'll refund the cost, **of course**.*

We can use comment adverbs such as **definitely** and **obviously** to indicate how sure we are (11) and others such as **fortunately** and **seriously** to say how we feel (12).

   11 *I'll **definitely** call you tonight.* • ***Obviously**, someone forgot to lock the door.*

   12 ***Fortunately**, no one was injured in the crash.* • *We're **seriously** thinking about moving to the country.*

Others include **actually, apparently, certainly, frankly, honestly, no doubt, presumably, sadly**

A Rewrite each sentence with one pair of adverbs added in appropriate positions.

carefully / tomorrow, completely / yesterday, enough / really, too / very much

1 I forgot my brother's birthday.

....

2 The piano is large and our doorway isn't wide.

....

3 We enjoyed the trip, but it was expensive.

....

4 I'll read the report.

....

B Choose an ending (a–f) for each beginning (1–6) and add these adverbs.

angrily, casually, enough, extremely, of course, traditionally, carelessly, completely, even, individually, only, very

1 ...., families were large, (...)
2 There was .... one ticket left (...)
3 He did the test so ...., (...)
4 ...., each player is good, (...)
5 Although he was dressed ...., (...)
6 Because he was .... annoyed, (...)

a and everyone wanted it, ...
b he wasn't .... relaxed.
c but that's .... changed now.
d he started complaining ....
e but they don't play well ....
   as a team.
f he didn't .... finish part of it.

C Add these adverbs to this text.

actually, certainly, nervously, probably, still, uncontrollably, apparently, completely, of course, seriously, very, unfortunately

"You've seen the ghost?" I asked.

"More than once," the elderly man replied. "(1) ...., I have a photograph. Want to see it?"

This is absurd, I thought, but asked, "You took a photo of the ghost?"

"No, not me. It's a photo of Lady Barnett from an old newspaper report of her death. She's wearing a long white gown, almost (2) .... the same one she wears when she appears at night." He said all this (3) .... (4) .... as if it was solid evidence for the truth of his ghostly tale. "She was rich and, (5) .... for her, she was murdered for her money. It all happened about 10 years ago. The police thought it was her husband who did it. He disappeared soon after. They found him later, locked in a small basement room. His hair had turned (6) .... white and his eyes were wide open. He was dead, (7) .... He was clutching the key to Lady Barnett's safety deposit box. I think her ghost had (8) .... found him and had scared him to death."

"Oh, my goodness! And she-she-she's still here?" I found myself stuttering (9) ....

"Oh, yes. I think she (10) .... walks through the house in search of his mistress. She only appears when there's a new woman in the house. (11) .... her husband was in love with another woman and he just wanted Lady Barnett's money so he could run away with her."

"What happened to the mistress?" I asked very (12) ...., looking round the dark room.

"Nobody knows," he answered. "But if I were her, I would stay far away from this house."

Equatives, comparatives, and superlatives

Equatives

Equatives are marked by **as … as** or **not as … as**. We use adjectives and adverbs in equatives to say that a person (1), thing (2), or action (3) is similar (or not) to another in some way.

1 *She's **as** tall **as** her father. • I'm **as** hungry **as** a horse. • He's **not as** young **as** he looks.*
2 *The van was **as** big **as** a house. • His new book is **not as** interesting **as** his other one.*
3 *I came **as** soon **as** possible. • Write **as** fast **as** you can. • It did**n't** do **as** well **as** we had hoped.*
 (NOT ~~She's as tall her father. Write fast as you can. It didn't do well we had hoped.~~)

We can use focus adverbs such as **just** and **only** before equatives (4). We sometimes use **not so … as** for the negative (5).

4 *Our plan is **just as** good **as** theirs. • You're **only as** old **as** you feel. • He's **not even as** tall **as** she is.*
5 *This year's harvest wasn't **so** bad **as** last year's. • He's **not so** arrogant **as** he used to be.*

Note the use of equatives with a singular noun: *He's not **as good a teacher as** Mrs. Mahoney.*
(NOT ~~He's not as good teacher as Mrs. Mahoney. He's not as a good teacher as her.~~)

Comparatives

We change adjectives and adverbs to say that a person (6), a thing (7), or an action (8) has more or less of a quality **than** another. We put **more** or **less** before long forms and add **-er** to short forms.

6 *She's **more** intelligent **than** he is. She's also **more** interesting. • He's slow**er than** a snail.*
7 *Some ideas are **less** practical **than** others. • His apartment is small**er** and cheap**er than** ours.*
8 *I should practise **more** often. • She always finishes her work **faster** than I do.*

We can treat adjectives such as **friendly** or **quiet** as either long forms (9) or short forms (10).

9 *Our neighbours have become **more friendly** recently. • The boys seem **more quiet** than usual.*
10 *Everyone was **friendlier** this time. • My new office is **quieter** than the old one.*

Others include **crazy, likely, lonely, narrow, simple, yellow**

We use special forms for the comparative of **good/well** and **bad/badly** (11). We use **further** (from **far**) for distance and when we mean "additional" (12). **Farther** is only used for distance.

11 *I thought the weather would be **better** in July, but it actually got **worse**.*
12 *How much **further/farther** do we have to walk? • We hope to get **further** details of the plan soon.*

We can use comparative forms, repeated with **and**, to emphasize that something is increasing or decreasing (13). We use **the** + comparative … **the** + comparative to say that one development is connected to another (14).

13 *We meet **more and more** frequently. • It's **less and less** common. • Alice got **taller and taller**.*
14 ***The sooner** we leave, **the faster** we'll get there. • **The older** I get, **the crazier** everything seems.*

Superlatives

We can use adjectives and adverbs to say that people (15) or things and actions (16) have the most or least of a quality. We put **the most** or **the least** before long forms and add **-est** to short forms.

15 *He's **the most likely** to succeed. • It's **the least dangerous**.*
16 *Where's **the most beautiful** beach in the world? • That's **the simplest** question of all. •*
 ***The least popular** subject is algebra. • I was sure my golf ball had landed **nearest** to the hole.*

Note the special forms for **good/well** (**best**), **bad/badly** (**worst**) and **far** (**farthest/furthest**).

After superlatives we use **in** or **on**, not **of**, before singular words for groups (17) or places (18).

17 *Raj is **the youngest** student **in** the class. • I'm **the tallest in** my family.*
18 *He's **the best** player **in** the world. • I think we stayed in **the worst** hotel **on** the island.*
 (NOT ~~He's the best player of the world.~~)

A Write the most appropriate forms of adjectives and adverbs from one set in each sentence.

bad / skilled / well early / new / well-behaved easy / short / well-known
beautiful / different /quick fast / old / tall good / likely / long

1 The .... you wait, the .... you are to miss the ....
 bargains in the sale.
2 Our .... son is .... than his dad, but our other two haven't grown
 as ....
3 The .... group of students is .... than that other group who stayed
 here ....
4 His .... book is .... and .... to read than all the
 others.
5 There are several .... ways to get to the .... beach on the other side
 of the island, but the .... way is by boat.
6 I can't play as .... as most of the others, but I'm not the .... player
 or the .... of all those who want to participate.

B Complete the first paragraph of an essay about fast food with these adjectives and adverbs.

better, puzzled, as quickly as, more easily, the best, faster, smaller, less beneficial, more wasteful,
the most important

When did we decide that "more convenient" is (1) .... way to choose between
two different things to eat? Why do people now want food (2) .... possible, in
containers that are (3) .... thrown away? How did "(4) ....
is (5) ...." become our slogan? Don't we see that this is
(6) .... and much (7) .... than making our own food?
Is it because we want food to have a much (8) .... place in our lives?
But isn't food one of (9) .... things? Am I the only one who is
(10) .... by this?

C Correct the mistakes in this text.

In one experiment, students were asked to look at photographs of people and choose the ~~good~~ best
words and phrases to describe them. The students didn't know that the researchers had chosen the
photographs to represent two groups. In Group A, they put the good-looking of all the people whose
photographs were used. For Group B, they chose people who (they decided) were not attractive as
those in Group A. According to the students, the people in Group A were warm, kind, exciting, and
sensitive than those in Group B. Also, Group A would find high-paid jobs, have successful marriages,
and lead happy lives than Group B. The women in Group A were considered to have appealing
personalities and to be socially skilled than the Group B women, but also to be vain, materialistic,
snobbish, and likely to get divorced than them. Interestingly, the students decided that Group A
would be bad parents than Group B.

Prepositions of movement and place

From, to, toward

We use **from** for the origin or starting point of movement and **to** for the goal or end point (1). More figuratively, **from** and **to** can be used for the starting and end points of changes (2).

   1 *We flew straight **from** Toronto **to** San Francisco. • I can walk **from** my apartment **to** work.*

   2 *He translated the book **from** Russian **to** English. • It went **from** very cool **to** very hot in an hour.*

We can use **toward** ("in the direction of") to focus on the direction of movement (3). More figuratively, **toward** can be used to talk about the direction of development or change (4).

   3 *I suddenly saw a car coming **toward** me. • If you get lost, try to walk **toward** the south.*

   4 *The trend is **toward** much larger farms. • This agreement is an important step **toward** peace.*

Note that **towards** is also used. *It's a step towards peace.*

Into and onto

We can use **into** when we focus on movement to a place inside something (5) and **onto** for movement to a surface of some kind (6).

   5 *We took a bus **into** the city. • The waiter poured some wine **into** each glass.*

   6 *Let's move the small books **onto** the top shelf. • Paint was dripping from his brush **onto** the floor.*

Across, over, through

We can use **across**, **over**, and **through** for movement from one side of something to the other.

   7 *The explorers had to get **across/over/through** the Rocky Mountains to reach the coast.*

We usually use **across** for movement to the other side of a surface or area (8), **over** for movement to the other side of something that is viewed as high or as a line (9), and **through** for movement that enters and leaves something (10).

   8 *We spent a month travelling **across** Canada. • She pushed a note **across** the table to him.*

   9 *The gate was locked so I climbed **over** the wall. • It was a good shot, but it went **over** the bar.*

   10 *You have to go **through** the kitchen to get to the bathroom. • The Saint John flows **through** Fredericton.*

We can use **across** and **over** for place ("on the other side of"): *There's a café **across** the street.*

Along and past

We can use **along** for movement in one direction or to describe the position of something which is somewhere in that direction (11). We can use **past** for movement beyond a specific point or to describe the position of something beyond a specific point (12).

   11 *I like walking **along** country lanes. • There's a café **along** the street.*

   12 *We drove **past** Surrey, but didn't stop there. • There's a café just **past** the library.*

Off and out of

We can use **off** for movement away from a surface or to describe the position of something in relation to a surface (13). We use **out of** for movement from the inside of something or to describe the position of something which is no longer inside (14).

   13 *Could you take that box **off** the table? • The platform was about two feet **off** the ground.*

   14 *I lifted the kitten **out of** the box. As soon as it was **out of** the box, it started crying.*

Note that we don't use **out** (without **of**) as a preposition. (NOT ~~It was out the box.~~)

More figuratively, **off** can be used with the sense of "not connected to" (15) and **out of** with the sense of "no longer having" (16).

   15 *This part of your essay is completely **off** the main topic. • Melville is an island **off** the west coast.*

   16 *We're **out of** milk, so I have to go to the store. • A lot of people are **out of** work now.*

A Complete the directions with these prepositions.

across, along, from, out of, past, to (×2), toward

Hilal (talking on the phone): Hi, Angie, it's me again. I'm sorry to bother you, but I'm in the post office and I can't remember how to get (1) .... the Red Lion (2) .... here.

Angie: That's okay. The Red Lion is on King Street, so when you're (3) .... the post office, you should turn right and walk (4) .... the cathedral. Go (5) ....
Diefenbaker Street and turn left when you reach Trudeau Street. Walk (6) ....
Trudeau Street (7) .... King Street and turn right.
The Red Lion will be on your right just (8) .... the library.

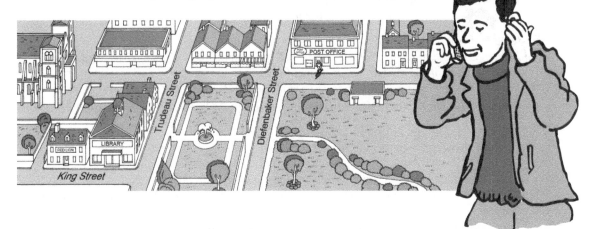

B Using a dictionary if necessary, add one pair of prepositions to each sentence.

along / toward, out of / from, through / to

1 When you go via a particular place, you go .... that place on your way
   .... another place.
2 When you're going up or down a road, you're going .... it .... one
   end of it.
3 When you're asked to wait outside a room, you have to be .... the room, but you
   must not move too far .... it.

C Add these prepositions to the following paragraphs from the beginning of *The English Patient*.

along, from, into, on, over, through, towards (×2)

She stands up in the garden where she has been working and looks into the distance. She has sensed a shift in the weather. There is another gust of wind, a buckle of noise in the air, and the tall cypresses sway. She turns and moves uphill (1) .... the house, climbing (2) ....
a low wall, feeling the first drops of rain (3) .... her bare arms. She crosses the loggia and quickly enters the house.

In the kitchen she doesn't pause but goes (4) .... it and climbs the stairs which are in darkness and then continues (5) .... the long hall, at the end of which is a wedge of light (6) .... an open door.

She turns (7) .... the room which is another garden—this one made up of trees and bowers painted over its walls and ceiling. The man lies on the bed, his body exposed to the breeze, and he turns his head slowly (8) .... her as she enters.

Prepositions used for connections or exceptions

Of and with

We use **of** and **with** when we talk about people and things being connected. We can put **of** between two noun phrases to show that the first belongs to or is part of the second (1). We can put **with** between two noun phrases when the second is a particular feature of the first (2).

> 1 *The roof **of** their house is bright red.* • *The sleeves **of** this shirt are too long.*
> 2 *Theirs is the house **with** the bright red roof.* • *I'm looking for a white shirt **with** short sleeves.*

We can use **of** to say how people are related (3) and **with** to say that people or things are together (4).

> 3 *Is Katelyn the daughter **of** Shauna Vargas? ~ Yes, she's a good friend **of** mine.*
> 4 *I think Ming went shopping **with** her friends.* • *Would you like some wine **with** your meal?*

We use **of** after some adjectives (5) and **with** after others (6).

> 5 *Marvin is **afraid of** dogs.* • *The report was **full of** mistakes.* (NOT ~~It was full with mistakes.~~) •
>   *Are you **aware of** the risks involved?* • *I was **fond of** my old car, but it had too many problems.*
> 6 *We were **faced with** a difficult choice.* • *I wasn't **familiar with** that computer program.* •
>   *There are side effects **associated with** most medications.* • *He wasn't **satisfied with** my work.*

With and by

We can use **with** plus a determiner and noun for the specific thing used to perform an action (7). We usually use **by** plus a noun (no determiner) or gerund when we want to describe the action in a more general way (8).

> 7 *I paid **with** my credit card.* • *The thief broke the lock **with** a knife.* (NOT ~~by a knife~~)
> 8 *I paid **by** credit card.* • *He opened the door **by** breaking the lock.* (NOT ~~by break the lock~~)

Other **by**-phrases used with a general meaning include **by air, by bus, by email, by phone**

A Complete each sentence with one pair of words or phrases (not necessarily in this order) plus *by*, *of*, or *with* where necessary.

a credit card / the yellow lampshade	the door / a screwdriver	American history / reading
her / taxi	~~any problems / the way~~	ours / some friends

▶ We weren't aware of .... any problems .... until we started getting complaints
from people who clearly weren't satisfied .... with the way ....
their new computers were working.

1 He tried to remove the old broken handle ....

2 I'm becoming more familiar .... about the Civil War.

3 We went out to dinner ....

4 They don't allow dogs on the bus so Khalida always goes .... whenever
she wants to take her dog ....

5 I wanted to buy that lamp .... but I didn't have enough cash
and they wouldn't let me pay for it ....

Except (for), besides, apart from

We can use **except** or **except for** ("not including") with someone or something not included in a general statement, usually after a quantifier such as **every** (9). We usually use **except for** (not **except**) with information added to a specific statement that makes it not completely true (10).

9 *It's open every day **except (for)** Sunday.* • *Everyone liked the movie **except** me.*

10 *She says she's stopped drinking coffee **except for** an occasional cup on weekends.*

We can use **except** (not **except for**) before preposition phrases (11) and clauses (12).

11 *I work here all day **except** on Friday.* • *It will be sunny everywhere **except** in Halifax.*

12 *I've never heard their baby cry **except** when it gets tired.*

In negative sentences, we can use **besides** with the same meaning as **except** (**for**) (13). In other sentences, **besides** usually means "in addition to" (14).

13 *I didn't know anyone in Montreal **besides/except (for)** my uncle Henri.*

14 ***Besides** lacrosse, what other sports do you like?* • *I've talked to a lot of people **besides** Guillaume.*

We can use **apart from** instead of **except** (**for**) ("not including") or **besides** ("in addition to").

15 *It's open every day **apart from** Sunday.* • ***Apart from** lacrosse, what other sports do you like?*

Note that **aside from** is used like **apart from**.

Without and minus

We use **except** (**for**) with something not included in a general statement. We use **without** for something not included in the wider senses of "not having" (16) or "not doing" something (17). We can use **minus** when we want to emphasize that something has been removed (18).

16 *I prefer coffee **without** sugar, don't you?* • *Romeo chose death rather than life **without** Juliet.*

17 *Bill changed his travel plans **without** any explanation. Then he left **without** saying goodbye.*

18 *They eventually published the report, **without/minus** several important sections.*

B **Using a dictionary if necessary, complete each sentence with a noun and a preposition.**

bread	fruit	meal	pizza
fish	ice cream	omelettes	rice

besides	except for	with
except (×2)	minus	without (×2)

1 We don't usually eat much .... when we have Indian food.

2 My grandfather liked to say that you can't make .... breaking eggs.

3 I first learned how to cook salmon and now I cook a lot of other .... that.

4 They usually drink wine with their evening .... this week.

5 My children don't eat a lot of .... bananas at breakfast.

6 Would you like some .... your strawberries?

7 We won't be able to make .... flour.

8 It was obvious that someone had already decided it was time to start eating because on the table was our ...., ... one very large slice.

Phrasal verbs

Words such as **in** or **on** that are used as prepositions before noun phrases (1) can also be used as particles after verbs (2). We can also use other words such as **away, back,** or **out** as particles (3). These verb + particle combinations (**sleep in, go out**) are called two-word verbs or phrasal verbs.

    1 *I usually drink coffee **in the morning**. • He said he left the keys **on the table**.*
    2 *I **slept in** this morning and missed my bus. • He **put on** his boots and parka.*
    3 *I tried to catch the dog, but it **ran away**. • When will she **come back**? • Did you **go out** last night?*
Other phrasal verbs include **fall over, get through, go ahead, sit down, stand up, take off**

Some phrasal verbs are used without an object (4) and others are used with an object. When the object is a noun phrase, we can usually put it before (5) or after the particle (6). When the object is a pronoun, we put it before the particle (7).

    4 *It's time to **get up**. • I wish these flies would **go away**. • **Watch out!*** (NOT ~~Watch out that!~~)
    5 *Don't **turn on** the light. You'll **wake up** the baby. • He **took off** his shoes.*
    6 *Don't **turn** the light **on**. You'll **wake** the baby **up**. • He **took** his shoes **off**.*
    7 *Don't **turn** it **on**. You'll **wake** him **up**. • He **took** them **off**.* (NOT ~~He took off them.~~)

After a phrasal verb we can also use a gerund (8) or a clause (9). We don't usually put clauses or very long phrases between the verb and the particle.

    8 *Have you **given up** drinking? • They told us to **keep on** working.* (NOT *... ~~to keep on work.~~*)
    9 *Andy **pointed out** that we didn't have enough time. • You should **read over** what you've written.* (NOT ~~You should read what you've written over.~~)

We can use phrasal verbs with prepositions. These combinations of verb + particle + preposition are sometimes called three-word verbs. We put pronouns after the prepositions.

    10 *This book is valuable and you should **hold on to** it.* (NOT ~~hold on it hold it on to~~)
    *Go ahead and I'll **catch up with** you later.* (NOT ~~I'll catch up you I'll catch you up~~)
Others include **face up to, get around to, go along with, look forward to, watch out for**

We often use phrasal verbs such as **put off** or **leave out** in informal situations (11) rather than other verbs with similar meanings such as **postpone** or **omit** which may sound more formal (12).

    11 *Let's **put** the meeting **off** till next week. • Don't **leave out** the author's name.*
    12 *We should **postpone** the meeting until next week. • You must not **omit** the author's name.*

A Using a dictionary if necessary, rewrite the sentences in a more informal style, using appropriate forms of these phrasal verbs.

cut back on, fill in, give up, go in, send back, do away with, find out, go along with, go up, take off

1 You should complete this form and return it with your payment.
    You have to ....

2 The students have abandoned their attempt to get the province to abolish tuition fees.
    The students ....

3 It was necessary to reduce our spending after we discovered that our rent was increasing.
    We had to ....

4 Please observe local customs at the mosque and remove your shoes before entering.
    Please ....

B Complete the text with appropriate phrasal verbs using these verbs and particles.

bend, breathe (×2), go, lift, push, raise, stand, away, back, down, in, out, up (×3)

When you have to spend a lot of time sitting at a desk, it is important to take short breaks and stretch your neck and back. You can use this exercise to help you stretch.

   (1)..................................... your chair to the side and stand up, making sure there is some space in front of you. (2)................................... straight, with your arms hanging loosely by your side.

   Breathe in deeply as you (3)..................... your arms .... over your head. Pause a moment.

   Then (4)................................... slowly as you swing your arms forward, letting them fall as you (5)..................... your whole body .... until your hands are near your feet. Pause a moment.

   Then, (6)............................. as you (7)..................... your body .... very slowly, beginning with your hips, then your upper body, followed by your head and arms.

   Repeat the exercise at least once before you (8)................................... to your desk again.

C Choose A, B, or both as appropriate sentences to use in this dialogue.

   Ani: What's the meaning of "reimburse"?
1 Raz: I don't know. (A) Let's look up it in the dictionary. (B) Let's look it up in the dictionary.
2 Ani: (A) Hand over the dictionary and I'll do it. (B) Hand it over the dictionary and I'll do it.
3 Raz: (A) I left behind it at home this morning. (B) I left it behind at home this morning.
4   (A) I think I put down beside my computer. (B) I think I put it down beside my computer. Okay, so we can't use a dictionary. What's the context?
   Ani: It says, "They reimbursed his tuition fees."
5 Raz: (A) Maybe it means they figured out what his tuition was.
       (B) Maybe it means they figured what his tuition was out.
6 Ani: (A) But then it says he paid off some debts. (B) But then it says he paid off some.
7 Raz: (A) Maybe it means to pay back money to someone.
       (B) Maybe it means to pay money back to someone.
8 Ani: (A) So, they gave back him the money for his tuition.
       (B) So, they gave him back the money for his tuition.
   Raz: Sounds good to me.

Complex infinitives and gerunds

Complex infinitives

Instead of the simple infinitive (1), we can use the perfect infinitive (**to have** + past participle) when we want to be clear that we're talking about an earlier time or a completed action (2).

    1 *Ali seems **to be** sick a lot.* • *I'm hoping **to read** the guidebook before we get to Vancouver.*
    2 *Ali seems **to have been** sick a lot.* • *I'm hoping **to have read** the guidebook before we get to Vancouver.*

We can use the perfect infinitive after **would** plus **like**, **hate**, **love**, or **prefer** when we refer to earlier events (3). We can also use the simple infinitive after **would have liked**, etc. with a similar meaning (4). We sometimes use the perfect forms of both verbs in informal situations (5).

    3 *I would like **to have been** there.* • *You would hate **to have seen** all the destruction.*
    4 *I would have liked **to be** there.* • *You would have hated **to see** all the destruction.*
    5 *I would have liked **to have been** there.* • *You would have hated **to have seen** it.*

We can use the progressive infinitive (**to be** + present participle) for an action in progress (6) and the perfect progressive infinitive (**to have been** + present participle) for an action in progress at an earlier time (7).

    6 *The children will pretend **to be sleeping**.* • *The girl seemed **to be waiting** for someone.*
    7 *They'll pretend **to have been sleeping**.* • *She seemed **to have been waiting** there for hours.*

We can use the passive infinitive (**to be** + past participle) for present or future actions happening to the subject (8) and the perfect passive infinitive (**to have been** + past participle) for earlier actions (9).

    8 *My computer is supposed **to be repaired** today.* • *The movers want **to be paid** in cash.*
    9 *It was supposed **to have been repaired** last week.* • *They were hoping **to have been paid** already.*

Complex gerunds

Instead of the simple gerund (10), we can use the perfect gerund (**having** + past participle) when we want to be clear that the action was in the past (11).

    10 *Kirsten regretted **telling** us about the money.* • *We thanked them for **supporting** us.*
    11 *She regretted **having told** us about the money.* • *We thanked them for **having supported** us.*

We can use the passive gerund (**being** + past participle) for an action that happens to the subject (12) and the perfect passive gerund (**having been** + past participle) to emphasize that the action happened in the past (13).

    12 *In her book, Matisa wrote about **being punished** as a child for speaking Cree.*
    13 *She still has nightmares from **having been separated from** her parents.*

A **Complete these sentences with *to be, being, to have,* or *having*.**

▶ I didn't mind ......*being*...... the youngest in a family of 10, but I knew I really wanted ......*to have*...... a large living space all to myself when I got older.

1 I'm supposed .... studying today, but I'm too tired from not .... slept at all last night.

2 You wouldn't like .... been living here during the ice storm, with the bridges being closed and the power .... out for weeks.

3 The original building is believed .... been constructed in 1870. It has always had structural problems from not .... been built on more solid ground.

4 The cleaners want .... finished their work in this room before they leave today because there are another two rooms on the second floor that have .... done tomorrow.

B Complete this table with appropriate examples of verbs from the completed sentences in part A at the bottom of page 60.

> ▶ Simple infinitive: **to** + base form of the verb (**to play**): ....to have......
>
> 1 Perfect infinitive: **to have** + past participle (**to have played**):
> ....
>
> 2 Progressive infinitive: **to be** + present participle (**to be playing**):
> ....
>
> 3 Perfect progressive infinitive: **to have been** + present participle (**to have been playing**):
> ....
>
> 4 Passive infinitive: **to be** + past participle (**to be played**):
> ....
>
> 5 Perfect passive infinitive: **to have been** + past participle (**to have been played**):
> ....
>
> ▶ Simple gerund: base form of the verb + **-ing** (**playing**): ....being........
>
> 6 Perfect gerund: **having** + past participle (**having played**):
> ....
>
> 7 Passive gerund: **being** + past participle (**being played**):
> ....
>
> 8 Perfect passive gerund: **having been** + past participle (**having been played**):
> ....

C Complete each sentence, using an infinitive or a gerund, in such a way that it is as similar as possible in meaning to the sentence above it.

1 You were supposed to do your homework before you went out.
Your homework ....

2 She had taken the time to help me and I wanted to thank her for that.
I wanted ....

3 They hadn't been told about the changes and complained about it.
They complained about ....

D Complete the text with these infinitives and gerunds.

to be burning, being held, to have visited, to have been based, to be using, meeting,
not to have seen, to have been built, travelling, to have been doing

Did Marco Polo tell the truth when he wrote about (1) .... to China and
(2) .... the emperor Kublai Khan? Or did the 13th-century Italian explorer just make
up stories about places he would like (3) .... and things he would like
(4) .... instead of (5) .... captive in prison?
According to some experts, his stories appear (6) .... on things he had
heard about rather than things he had seen himself. In his account, the Chinese were said
(7) .... paper money and (8) .... "large black stones"
(coal) for heat long before Europeans. However, the Great Wall is known (9) ....
before his travels, yet he appears (10) .... it.

Adjectives, nouns, and pronouns with infinitives and gerunds

Adjectives used with infinitives only

We can use infinitives, not gerunds, after some adjectives when we talk about being certain (**sure**) or willing (**eager**) to do something (1) and about our feelings or reactions (**glad, delighted**) (2).

    1 *The children are **sure to get up** early tomorrow. They're **eager to go** to the beach.*

    2 *I'm **glad to meet** you. • I was **delighted to hear** the good news about your scholarship.*

Other adjectives used like this include **disappointed, happy, pleased, sad, sorry, surprised**

After some adjectives, we can use **for** with a noun phrase or pronoun to identify the subject of the infinitive (3). We can use **of** (not **for**) when we are evaluating someone's action (4).

    3 *It was **good for the children to visit** their grandparents.* (The children had a good experience.)

    4 *It was **good of the children to visit** their grandparents.* (The children acted in a good way.)

Other adjectives used like this include **bad, nice, silly, stupid, wrong**

We often use infinitives after **too** + an adjective, or an adjective + **enough**.

    5 *Is the coffee still **too hot** (for you) **to drink**? • The small bags are **light enough** (for us) **to carry**.*

Adjectives used with infinitives or gerunds

After empty subject **it** + **be** and adjectives such as **nice** and **difficult**, we can use an infinitive (6) or a gerund (7), with little difference in meaning. When we make the object of the infinitive our topic as the subject of the sentence, we use an infinitive after these adjectives (8).

    6 *It was really **nice to talk** to Xuemei. • Was it very **difficult to learn** Arabic?*

    7 *It was really **nice talking** to Xuemei. • Was it very **difficult learning** Arabic?*

    8 ***Xuemei** was really **nice to talk** to. • Was **Arabic** very **difficult to learn**?*

Other adjectives used like this include **easy, exciting, great, hard, impossible, interesting**

We can use gerunds as subjects before **be** plus adjectives such as **important** and **necessary** (9). After empty subject **it** + **be** and these adjectives, we use infinitives (10).

    9 ***Listening** carefully is **important**, but **writing** everything down isn't **necessary**.*

    10 *It's **important to listen** carefully, but it isn't **necessary to write** everything down.*

Other adjectives used like this include **crucial, essential, unnecessary, vital**

After an adjective such as **anxious**, we can use an infinitive or a preposition plus a gerund with different meanings (11). After many adjectives, we can only use a preposition and gerund (12).

    11 *I was **anxious to leave**.* (I was eager.) *• I was **anxious about leaving**.* (I was worried.)

    12 *J.K. Gulley is **famous for inventing** the Gulley Hook.* (NOT ~~He's famous to invent it.~~)

       *Isn't Lucia **capable of doing** it by herself?* (NOT ~~Isn't Lucia capable to do it by herself?~~)

A **Complete each sentence, using an infinitive or gerund, in such a way that it is as similar as possible in meaning to the sentence above it.**

1 Planning ahead is essential in my job.

    It's ....

2 Jessica didn't see any of her friends at the mall and she was disappointed.

    Jessica was disappointed ....

3 Christopher was so good to come to our rescue when our car broke down.

    It was so good ....

4 It isn't easy driving those huge buses along narrow winding roads.

    Those huge buses ....

Nouns and pronouns used with infinitives only

We can use infinitives after certain nouns with meanings similar to verbs taking infinitives (e.g. **agree—agreement**) (13). We can use these nouns as subjects with **be** before an infinitive, or after empty subject **it** + **be** before an infinitive (14). In these structures we can also use nouns such as **ambition** and **goal** with infinitives to talk about future actions (15).

13 *We **agreed to share** the cost.* • *We had an **agreement to share** the cost.*
14 *The **agreement was to share** the cost.* • *It was our **agreement to share** the cost.*
15 *Our **goal is to save** $2000 by next summer.* • *It's his **ambition to become** an astronomer.*
Other nouns used like this include **aim, decision, desire, expectation, hope, offer, plan, wish**

We can use infinitives after general nouns for people and things such as **person** or **place** (16), or after indefinite pronouns and adverbs such as **someone** and **nowhere** (17). We do this when we talk about what we can or want to do with those people and things. After nouns and indefinite pronouns, we can use **for** with a noun phrase or object pronoun to identify the subject of the infinitive (18).

16 *Miguel's the **person to ask** about graphics.* • *St. John's is a great **place to visit**.* • *I brought **a book to read**.*
17 *He needs **someone to love**.* • *Is there **anything to eat**?* • *They have **nowhere to go** at night.*
18 *It's **time for the kids to go** to bed.* • *There's **nothing for us to do**.* • *I brought **a book for you to read**.*

Nouns and pronouns used with infinitives or gerunds

We don't usually use gerunds directly after nouns, except after a few phrases such as **have a problem** and **it's no use** (19). After nouns such as **interest** and **talent**, we can use a preposition plus a gerund (20). We often use a structure with **the** + noun (**the cost**) and **of** + gerund (**of living**) (21).

19 *Did you have **a problem finding** the place?* • *It was **no use complaining** because no one cared.*
20 *Will had a **talent for acting**.* • *I had no **interest in studying**.* (NOT ~~I had no interest to study.~~)
21 ***The cost of living** in Toronto is very high.* • ***The thought of eating** eggs makes me feel queasy.* • *He stressed **the importance of being** on time.* • *I don't like **the idea of (you) going** alone.*

After nouns such as **attempt** and **intention** we can use infinitives or prepositions plus gerunds with little difference in meaning (22). When we talk about the use or purpose of something, we can use a noun or indefinite pronoun with an infinitive (23) or **for** with a gerund (24). There is no difference in meaning.

22 *His **attempt to break/at breaking** the record failed.* • *I have **no intention to leave/of leaving**.*
23 *They have a **machine to clean** carpets.* • *I need to find **something to remove** stains.*
24 *They have a **machine for cleaning** carpets.* • *I need to find **something for removing** stains.*

B **Add one combination of noun/pronoun plus a verb as an infinitive or gerund in each space.**

cost / rent, information / reserve, plan / take, someone / ask, idea / study, place / stay, problem / keep, task / call

Leila was both excited and nervous about the (1) .... of .... in Ottawa during the summer. Her (2) .... was .... only two courses at the university because she didn't want to have a (3) .... up with the lectures and assignments. She had heard that the most convenient (4) .... was in the student residence, but they hadn't sent her any (5) .... about .... a room there. So, her next (6) .... was .... and find (7) .... about the kind of accommodation they had and the (8) .... of .... one of their rooms during the summer months.

Reporting statements and questions

Reporting statements

In formal uses, we usually include **that** after reporting verbs when we report a statement (1), but in informal uses we often omit **that** (2).

    1 *The prime minister said **that** she would consider it.* • *The police report **that** crime is down.*
    2 *She said _ she'd think about it.* • *I told him _ I was leaving.* • *He agreed _ it was a good idea.*

We usually include **that** after verbs that describe the speaker's intention (**complain, deny**, etc.) (3), the manner of speaking (4), phrasal verbs (5), and when we include other information between the reporting verb and the **that**-clause (6).

    3 *They **complained that** they had been left out.* • *He **denied that** he was responsible.*
    4 *She **whispered that** she had to go.* • *The man **shouted that** he was innocent.*
    5 *One student **pointed out that** the date was wrong.* • *She **called out that** dinner was ready.*
    6 *He said in last week's meeting **that** we were wrong.* • *We agree with the critics **that** it's old.*

We can use nouns such as **announcement** and **response** before a **that**-clause containing indirect speech to report statements. After these nouns, we usually include **that**.

    7 *"Classes are cancelled."* → *Did you hear the **announcement that** classes were cancelled?*
    8 *"I worked hard."* → *His **response that** he worked hard isn't true.* (NOT ~~His response he worked~~ ...)
Other nouns used like this include **argument, claim, comment, explanation, report, statement**

We can also report statements by using a noun with **be** and a **that**-clause containing indirect speech.
    9 *"It'll cost a lot."* → *Her only **comment was that** it would cost a lot.*

Reporting questions

We begin reported questions (or indirect questions) with **wh**-words (10), **if**, or **whether** (11).
    10 *"Who is she?"* → *He asked **who** she was.* • *"What does she do?"* → *He asked **what** she did.*
    11 *"Is she a doctor or a nurse?"* → *He wanted to know **if/whether** she was a doctor or a nurse.*

We form indirect questions with the subject before the verb and no question mark (12). We don't change the word order when a **wh**-word is the subject of the question (13).
    12 *"Where are the keys?"* → *I asked **where** the keys **were**.* (NOT ~~I asked where were the keys?~~)
    13 *"Who has the keys?"* → *I asked **who had** the keys.* (NOT ~~I asked who the keys had.~~)

We can report some **wh**-questions with **should** (about the right thing to do) by using an infinitive.
    14 *"When should I come and what should I do?"* → *I asked them **when to come** and **what to do**.*
Note that **why** is not used in this way: *I asked them why I should do it.* (NOT ... ~~why to do it.~~)

We begin indirect yes/no questions with **if** or **whether**.
    15 *"Are you a nurse?"* → *I asked **if / whether** she was a nurse.* (NOT ~~I asked if was she a nurse?~~)

We use **whether** (not **if**) after a preposition (16), before an infinitive (17), and after the verb **question** (18). **Whether or not** can be used as a phrase, but not **if or not** (19).
    16 *"Is it okay to use a dictionary?"* → *Someone inquired **about whether** it was okay to use a dictionary.* (NOT ~~Someone inquired about if it was okay to use a dictionary.~~)
    17 *"Should I wait for him?"* → *She's wondering **whether to wait** for him.* (NOT ... ~~if to wait for him.~~)
    18 *"Are they really Mounties?"* → *The man **questioned whether** they were really Mounties.*
    19 *"Did he win or not?"* → *I asked **whether or not** he won.* (OR *I asked **whether/if** he won **or not**.*)

A **Complete each sentence using indirect speech in such a way that it is as similar as possible in meaning to the sentence above it.**

1 "I'm not guilty!" called out one of the defendants.
One ....

2 It really surprised us when she said she'd been in the Arctic for two years.
Her statement ....

3 The students' argument is that the cost of tuition has increased too much and I agree.
I agree ....

4 He claimed, "I'm not a thief!" but no one believed him.
No one believed his ....

B **Choose an ending (a–d) for each beginning (1–4) and add the words _that_, _where_, _whether_, or _who_.**

1 Some of them were arguing about (...)   a .... isn't here.
2 The teacher is trying to find out (...)   b .... the weather was going to be bad.
3 I asked another student (...)   c .... to leave or stay there for another day.
4 We heard one report (...)   d .... to find the library.

C **Rewrite these sentences after correcting the mistakes.**

1 One of the visitors asked about if will there be a fridge in the hotel room?
....

2 He asked me why to do that and I pointed out it was part of my job.
....

3 She asked me what do next and my response that she gets some more chairs.
....

4 Her explanation no one asked her if or not she has a degree was incredible.
....

D **Change these statements and questions to indirect speech and add them to the text.**

"There is a moster under my bed."   "Why aren't you sleeping?"   "Have you seen the monster?"
"I haven't, but I know it has big teeth."   "What is a 'moster'?"   "Where did it come from?"

One time when I was babysitting for some friends, their five-year-old daughter got out of bed and came into the living room. I asked her (1) ....
She climbed on to the sofa beside me and whispered (2) ....
.... I started to ask her (3) .... , then I
realized that she meant "monster." I asked her (4) ....
She said (5) ....
    I asked her (6) .... She didn't know, but it
had really big eyes and sharp teeth. We eventually both fell asleep on the sofa and, luckily for us, the monster stayed in the bedroom.

Reporting orders, requests, advice, and opinions

Reporting orders and requests

We usually report orders using **tell** with an object and an infinitive.

    1 "Don't touch it." → *He **told us not to** touch it.* • "Be quiet!" → *She **told everyone to** be quiet.*
Other less common verbs used to report orders include **command, direct, instruct, order**

We can also report orders in a **that**-clause with the modals **have to** or **must** (2). After verbs such as
demand and **insist**, a subjunctive is sometimes used (3).

    2 "Stop arguing!" → *Their mother told them that they **had to/must** stop arguing.*
    3 "Do it yourself!" → *He insisted that I **had to do** it myself.* OR *He insisted that I **do** it myself.*

We usually report requests using **ask** with an object and an infinitive (4). When we report requests by
speakers about their own actions, we don't include an object before the infinitive (5).

    4 "Please don't smoke." → *I **asked him not to** smoke.* • "Come in." → *He **asked me to** come in.*
    5 "May I leave?" → *She **asked to** leave.* • "Can I go?" → *He **asked to** go.* (NOT ~~He asked me to go.~~)
Other verbs used to report requests include **beg, plead with, request**

We can also report requests in an **if**-clause with the modals **could** or **would**.

    6 "Please help me." → *The old man asked (us) if we **could/would** help him.*

Reporting advice

We can report advice by using verbs such as **recommend** or **suggest** followed by a **that**-clause with
should (7) or a subjunctive in more formal uses (8). We can also use a gerund for the suggested
action when we don't want to mention who will perform the action (9).

    7 "You should go by train." → *He recommended that we **should go** by train.*
    8 "You should take the early train." → *He suggested that we **take** the early train.*
    9 "You should drive." → *He recommended **driving**.* (NOT ~~He recommended us driving.~~)

We can use the verb **advise** with an object and an infinitive (10) or with a **that**-clause or a
gerund (11).

    10 "Wait a few days." → *She advised **him to wait** a few days.* (NOT ~~She suggested him to wait.~~)
    11 *She advised (him) that he (**should**) **wait** a few days.* • *She advised **waiting** a few days.*

We can use different reporting verbs such as **remind** and **warn** with **that**-clauses to introduce
different kinds of reported advice.

    12 "A taxi will be much faster." → *She **reminded** him that a taxi **would** be much faster.*
    13 "You must be careful." → *She **warned** them that they **must/had to** be careful.*
We can also report a warning by using an infinitive: *She warned them **to be** careful.*

Reporting opinions

We use "thinking" verbs with **that**-clauses to report opinions.

    14 "Oh, it's nice!" → *She **thought** that it was nice.* • "I'll win." → *He **believes** that he'll win.*
Other verbs used like this include **expect, feel, imagine, reckon, suppose, suspect**

We can use the verbs **say** and **tell** in the progressive to report general opinions in informal situations.

    15 *The students **were saying** that the test was unfair.* • *Teachers **are telling** us there's a problem.*

We can also report opinions and feelings with nouns (16) and adjectives (17) before **that**-clauses.

    16 "Girls mature earlier than boys." → *It is her **view that** girls mature earlier than boys.*
Other nouns used like this include **belief, conclusion, diagnosis, hypothesis, opinion, theory**
    17 "It's a mistake." → *I was **sure** that it was a mistake.* OR *She is **certain** that it is a mistake.*
Other adjectives used like this include **aware, convinced, doubtful, positive, sorry, worried**

A Complete each sentence in such a way that it is as similar as possible in meaning to the sentence above it.

1 Professor to her students: "Please do not eat or drink during lectures."
The professor asked ....

2 Officer to the defendant: "Stand up when the judge comes in."
The officer ordered ....

3 Employee to his boss: "Can I leave early on Friday?"
The employee asked ....

4 Scott's mother to Scott: "You should apply to several universities."
Scott's mother recommended ....

B Change each piece of advice to an appropriate reported form and add it to the text.

"Place your napkin in your lap."   "Don't put a lot of food on your plate all at once."
"Don't rest your elbows on the table."   "Don't take more food until it is offered."
"Chew your food with your mouth closed." "Ask somebody."
"Don't talk with your mouth full."   "Please pass the salt."

My friend Shauna Kim and I were huddled beside the small radiator in her room, eating slices of pizza from a cardboard PizzaLand container. She was telling me about an old book she had been reading, called *Table Manners for Young Ladies*. It instructed the reader, when she is sitting at the table before the meal, (1) .... and
(2) ....
    It told her, while she is eating, (3) .... and
(4) .... Certain things were bad manners and the book advised her (5) .... and
(6) .... It also said that, when she needed something, such as salt, she (7) ....
(8) .... rather than reach across the table for it.
    "Ah, the good old days," she sighed as she reached into the box for another slice.

C Complete each sentence with an adjective or noun and a *that*-clause based on one of the direct speech sentences.

aware	diagnosis		"I lost my temper."	"Take the early flight to Regina."
positive	belief		"Dogs aren't allowed here."	"You will all pass the exam."
sorry	recommendation		"You have an ear infection."	"A perfect life can be achieved."

1 It was our dad's ....
2 Idealism is the ....
3 My doctor's .... was

....
4 Preema has calmed down and she's very ....
5 Our teacher was ....
6 The visitor obviously wasn't ....

Adjectives, the subjunctive, or **should** with noun clauses

Adjectives with noun clauses

We can use **that**-clauses (1) and **wh**-clauses (2) after adjectives. After some adjectives, such as **sorry** and **happy**, we include prepositions before **wh**-clauses, but not before **that**-clauses (3).

1 *Krishna was **surprised that** you asked about him.* • *It isn't **surprising that** the weather was bad.*
2 *We weren't **certain when** he would arrive.* • *Isn't it **amazing how much** teenagers can eat?*
3 *I'm **sorry about what** I said.* • *I'm **sorry that** I was late.* (NOT ~~I'm sorry about that I was late.~~)
  *We're happy **with how** it looks.* • *We're happy **that** it looks OK.* (NOT ~~We're happy how it looks.~~)

We can use empty subject **it** before a linking verb (**be, seem**) and an adjective plus a noun clause (4). In formal situations, the noun clause is sometimes used as subject (5).

4 ***It's disgraceful that** children can't spell their own names!* • ***It seems odd that** he didn't call.*
5 ***That children can't spell their own names** is disgraceful!* • ***That he didn't call** seems odd.*

In informal situations, we often use noun clauses without **that** after adjectives.

6 *I'm **sure** (that) it's a mistake.* • *We're **glad** (that) you're here.* • *He's **lucky** (that) he wasn't hurt.*

We can use adjectives for personal feelings (**afraid, worried**) before noun clauses describing the cause of those feelings (7). We can also use adjectives expressing degree of certainty (**positive, sure**) before noun clauses describing the information we are more or less certain about (8).

7 *We were **afraid** (that) you wouldn't come.* • *Aren't you **worried** (that) Arshad might get injured?*
Other adjectives used like this include **amazed, angry, disappointed, happy, proud, sad**

8 *He was **positive** (that) he had chosen the right answer.* • *I'm not **sure** if I heard him correctly.*
Other adjectives used like this include **certain, confident, convinced, doubtful, unsure**

A Rewrite these pairs of sentences as a single sentence containing a noun clause.

▶ He made such a mess. I was angry about it.   ...I was angry (that) he made such a mess....

1 Our old car might break down. We were afraid of that.
  We ....

2 Karen suddenly decided to quit her job. I was completely surprised by that.
  I ....

3 The test would be easy. Sean was absolutely sure of it.
  Sean ....

B Choose an adjective or an adjective with a preposition for each space. Add *that*, *how*, *what*, or *when* where necessary.

aware of, embarrassed by, glad, amazed, surprising, unlikely

Our teacher always encouraged us to try to guess what new words and phrases meant because it was (1) .... we would always be able to use our dictionaries. It was good advice, but I was very (2) .... wrong my guesses could be sometimes. For example, I had guessed that the phrase "kick the bucket" must mean that you are very happy and you show that you are happy by kicking a bucket. You just give it a good kick. That made sense to me. So, it was (3) .... I discovered that it meant the same as "die." I was really (4) .... I hadn't tried to use the phrase. I would be so (5) .... people would think if they had told me that they had good news and I had said, "Great! Now you'll kick the bucket!" They would be totally (6) .... I had said such an inappropriate thing.

The subjunctive or **should** in noun clauses

C **Write the numbers of appropriate examples in the spaces.**

We can use the present subjunctive, which has the same form as the base form of the verb, in
that-clauses   . We put **not** before the verb in the negative subjunctive   . We can use **should**
before the base form of the verb instead of the present subjunctive   .

  9 *Dr. Ali specifically requested that no one **have** access to patients' files unless authorized.*
 10 *We have already recommended that young children **not be** left alone in parked cars.*
 11 *The doctor requested that no one **should have** access to the files. • We have already recommended
     that children **shouldn't be** left alone.*

The past subjunctive (**were**) is also used in noun clauses after **wish**: *I wish (that) I were taller.*

We can use the present subjunctive or **should** in **that**-clauses after verbs expressing orders   ,
rules   , or suggestions   .

 12 *The committee <u>has suggested</u> that the cost of admission (**should**) **be** increased.*
 13 *The job description <u>stipulates</u> that the applicant (**should**) **have** a degree in English.*
 14 *The judge <u>insisted</u> that the boy (**should**) **be** punished and that he (**should**) **pay** for the damage.*

Other verbs used with the subjunctive include **advise, ask, demand, order, propose, require**

We can use the subjunctive or **should** in a reported order   , but not in a reported statement   .

 15 *"He has to be over 18." → They insist that he (**should**) **be** over 18.*
 16 *"I AM over 18!" → He insists that he **is** over 18.*

We can also use the subjunctive or **should** in **that**-clauses after nouns expressing orders   ,
rules   , or suggestions   and after adjectives expressing what is necessary   .

 17 *It is our <u>recommendation</u> that he (**should**) **not say** anything until the investigation is over.*
 18 *Isn't there a <u>rule</u> that safety equipment (**should**) **be** worn whenever machinery is running?*
 19 *They gave <u>instructions</u> that all passengers (**should**) **have** passports ready for inspection.*
 20 *It is <u>essential</u> that no one (**should**) **feel** excluded. It is <u>vital</u> that every voice (**should**) **be** heard.*

Other adjectives used like this include **crucial, imperative, important, necessary**

D **Choose an ending (a–f) for each beginning (1–6) and add appropriate forms of these
words, using the subjunctive or *should* where appropriate.**

arrest, give, insist, recommend, spend, suggestion, crucial, have, not disturb, requirement,
stipulate, wear

1 The nurse says it's .... (...)
2 The advertisement .... (...)
3 My friend .... (...)
4 Someone offered the .... (...)
5 The school had a .... (...)
6 The prisoner .... (...)

a that the winner .... a car as the prize.
b that uniforms .... at all times.
c that the applicant .... two years'
  experience.
d that the patient ....
e that the police .... the wrong person.
f that we .... a week in Paris.

Uses of noun clauses

Complex information in noun clauses

We can use noun clauses in a series to present complex information. We include **that** when we want to avoid ambiguity (e.g., to avoid "We have seen researchers" in the example below) or we can omit **that** to avoid repeating it too often (e.g. "people will believe they witnessed …").

1 *We have seen **that** researchers have been able to show **that** people will believe **(that)** they witnessed certain things because of information presented in police questions.*

We can also use several noun clauses in a list for a series of linked ideas (2) or alternatives (3).

2 *Bleck has argued **that** the long human childhood is needed for learning complex skills, **that** it allows children time to grow into many tasks, **and that** it is actually beneficial for parents.*

3 *It is clearly not true **that** students learn everything they are taught **or that** they know only what they are taught **or that** they can remember everything they are taught.*

We can include a phrase (4) or clause (5), separated by commas, after **that** in a noun clause. We put the first comma after **that**, not before it. We don't put commas around a **wh**-clause used as a subject after **that** (6).

4 *An important discovery was **that,** <u>in both types of environments</u>, **the children's language developed at the same rate.** (*NOT *~~An important discovery was, that in both types~~ …)*

5 *Some teachers believe **that,** <u>if students see or hear errors</u>, **they will learn those errors**.*

6 *The idea **that** <u>what you eat</u> **affects your long-term health** shouldn't really be a big surprise.*

The position of noun clauses

We usually put noun clauses at the end of sentences when they are objects, especially when they are long and contain a lot of information.

7 *It's usually assumed **that government officials speaking on important matters of national security are telling the truth**.*

We can use noun clauses in front position as a connection to information already given (8) or to repeat or rephrase old information before presenting new information (9).

8 *Five days after the earthquake, a woman was found alive under the ruins of her house. **That she had survived** was described as a miracle. **How she did it** no one knew.*

9 *Speakers continually design their linguistic messages on the basis of assumptions about what their hearers already know. **What a speaker assumes is true or is known by the hearer** can be described as a presupposition.*

We can use **The fact that** … with a noun clause in front position when we want to present information (including new information) as an established fact.

10 *Daniel's early years were spent with his parents, who are deaf. His only contact with spoken language was through television. **The fact that he couldn't speak English by the age of four** is evidence that children need more than simple exposure to language.*

We can use noun clauses in mid position to spell out details of a fact or idea (11). We can show that information is additional (and could be omitted) by putting it in a parenthetical noun clause separated by commas, dashes, or parentheses (12).

11 *It isn't hard to figure out how the widespread assumption **that women talk more than men** came to be one of our social myths.*

12 *The idea behind "Secret Santas" is for each person in a family or group to buy one present, "from Santa," for only one other person. This solution (**that you buy one present instead of 10 or 20**) helps to reduce the stress of Christmas as well as the cost.*

A Add one set of clauses to each paragraph (not necessarily in this order).

what happened that day / what they're thinking / who their best friends are
if women and men talk equally / people think / the women talked more
that men think / that they hear women / women talk a lot
that men get the impression / that women are less likely than men / that women never tell jokes

For women, the essence of friendship is talk, telling each other (1) ....
.... and feeling, and (2) .... When asked
(3) ...., most women name other women they regularly
talk to.

    Women can and do tell jokes. However, it is true (4) ....
to tell jokes in large groups, especially groups including men, so it's not surprising
(5) .... (6) ....

Studies have shown that, (7) .... in a group,
(8) .... (9) ....

The finding (10) .... (11) ....
.... may be due to the fact (12) .... talking in social
situations where men have little to say.

B Write one of these clauses in each space in the following sentences and add *that* where it is appropriate.

Columbus wasn't the first European   there was another world
Columbus reached Iceland   he could reach China
Columbus's visit to Iceland gave him the confidence   there would eventually be a place to land

Was it from the Vikings in Iceland that Christopher Columbus learned the crucial information
(1) .... further to the west?
Columbus's son described a voyage his father had made to the northern edge of Europe in 1477.
Many scholars now believe (2) ....
during that voyage. Seven years later, in 1484, Columbus proposed to the king of Portugal that, by
crossing the Atlantic, (3) ....
The idea (4) .... to reach America may come as a
surprise to some, but scholars in northern Europe have always suspected
(5) .... to set sail across the Atlantic,
knowing that, if he kept going, (6) ....
on the other side.

Reduced relative clauses

A relative clause formed with a participle and no relative pronoun is called a reduced relative clause. We use present participles (1) and past participles (2).

   1 There are two students <u>who are waiting outside</u>. → *There are two students **waiting outside**.*

   2 The strawberries <u>that had been dipped in chocolate</u> were really delicious! → *The strawberries **dipped in chocolate** were really delicious!*

We use a present participle in place of an active verb (3) and a past participle in place of a passive verb (4).

   3 There were teachers <u>who were shouting</u> and children <u>who were running</u> out of the building.
     → *There were teachers **shouting** and children **running** out of the building.*

   4 Aaron only drinks juice <u>that is made</u> from fresh fruit <u>that is grown</u> organically. → *Aaron only drinks juice **made** from fresh fruit **grown** organically.*

We can use participles instead of verbs referring to the past, present, or future.

   5 The winner is the person <u>who scored / scores / will score</u> the most points in the game.
     → *The winner is the person **scoring** the most points in the game.*

   6 First prize is for the most points <u>that were scored / are scored / will be scored</u> in the game.
     → *First prize is for the most points **scored** in the game.*

We can use a participle from a simple passive to describe a general situation (7), a progressive passive to emphasize that a situation is continuing (8), or a perfect passive to emphasize that a situation has continued from an earlier time (9).

   7 *We are concerned about people **held** in prison without a trial.* (= who are held)

   8 *We are concerned about people **being held** in prison without a trial.* (= who are being held)

   9 *We are concerned about people **having been held** in prison for years.* (= who have been held)

Participles can also be used in non-defining relative clauses, usually in written descriptions and narratives.

   10 *The old car, **trailing black smoke**, drove off toward town.* (= which was trailing smoke) •
     *Robert Mackenzie, **nicknamed "Big Bob,"** was my favourite teacher.* (= who was nicknamed)

We put **not** before the participle in negative reduced relative clauses.

   11 *My parents, **not having much money**, never went on vacation.* (= who didn't have) •
     *I'd prefer shirts **not made of polyester** if you have any.* (= which aren't made)

We can use some adjectives and adjective phrases after nouns in a way that is similar to reduced relative clauses.

   12 *There was one seat **available** on the flight.* (= one seat that was available) •
     *Mercury is a metal, **silver in colour**, often found in liquid form.* (= which is silver in colour)
Others include **necessary, possible, present, ready, responsible, suitable**

We don't use a participle instead of a verb that describes a single or sudden action (13) or a verb with a subject that is different from the relative pronoun (14).

   13 *There was a sudden bang **that woke me up**.* (NOT ~~There was a sudden bang waking me up.~~)

   14 *There are several things **that we need** from the store.* (NOT ~~There are several things needing ...~~) •
     *This isn't the information **that I was given** before.* (NOT ~~This isn't the information given before.~~)

We usually use an infinitive, not a participle, after a noun preceded by the adjectives **first, second**, etc.

   15 *Neil Armstrong was the first person **to walk** on the moon.* (= who walked on the moon)
     (NOT ~~Neil Armstrong was the first person walking on the moon.~~)

A Using a dictionary if necessary, complete these definitions with the nouns and appropriate forms of the verbs in reduced relative clauses.

puzzle, mermaid, cause, have, send, work, memo, shadow, cut, print, stand

1 A .... is a written note .... between people .... in the same organization.
2 A .... is an imaginary creature .... the body of a woman but a fish's tail instead of legs.
3 A .... is a picture .... on cardboard or wood and .... into various shapes that have to be fit together again.
4 A .... is a dark area on a surface .... by an object .... between direct light and that surface.

B Change each of these clauses to a reduced relative clause and write it in one of the spaces below.

it was standing on the bed	they are sitting in it
it is based on a true story	they didn't have children
it is parked outside	they went out to concerts and the theatre
it was covered with feathers	they were accused of crimes
it starts at 8 p.m.	they were committed during the war

1 There's a black car .... with two policemen ....
2 I found the puppy .... and .... from one of the pillows that it had ripped open.
3 The movie .... is a drama ....
4 Many people .... had to be set free because no witnesses could be found to testify against them.
5 We envied the Stossels. Paul and Monique Stossel, ..., were free to spend more of their time ....

C Make this text shorter by creating reduced relative clauses where possible.

For all you food lovers ~~who will be~~ sitting at home and who will be looking for something that is interesting on TV this afternoon, there's a fabulous new show that is called *The Asian Kitchen*, which has been created and which has been produced by Mary Sah, which begins at 4:30 this afternoon. Among the dishes that will be featured will be Saucy Tofu, which consists of tofu squares that have been dipped in a special batter, that have been deep-fried, and that have been covered in a creamy peanut sauce, and Evil Shrimp, which is made with hot peppers that have been sauteed with other vegetables, and that are served with shrimp that are sizzling in a shallow pool of red curry. It's the most delicious thing on TV today!

Possessives and pronouns with relative clauses; prepositions in relative clauses

A Write the numbers of appropriate examples in the spaces.

Possessives with relative clauses

We use **whose** instead of possessive determiners such as **his** before nouns. We usually use **whose** to refer to people ☐ , but it can also be used after nouns for organizations ☐ and places ☐ .

1 Is he the boy? <u>His</u> bag was stolen. → *Is he the boy **whose** bag was stolen?* (NOT ~~who his bag~~)
2 *Napa is in a region **whose** wines are famous.* • *Come to Jamaica, **whose** people welcome you.*
3 *Delco is a company **whose** products are everywhere.* • *That's the team **whose** coach was fired.*

We can also use **whose** to refer to things that are part of ☐ or belong to ☐ other things.

4 Draw a circle. <u>Its</u> radius is one inch. → *Draw a circle **whose** radius is one inch.*
5 *They live in a small town **whose** name I've forgotten.* (NOT ~~a small town which name~~)

Instead of **whose** before a noun, we can use **of which** after a noun when we talk about things ☐ . In informal uses, we can put **that** at the beginning and the noun plus **of** at the end ☐ .

6 *They live in a small town **that** I've forgotten the name **of**.*
7 *It's a small town, the name **of which** I've forgotten.* • *Draw a circle, the radius **of which** is one inch.*
In formal uses, **of which** is sometimes before the noun: *Draw a circle, of which the radius is …*

Pronouns with relative clauses

We can use relative clauses after personal pronouns ☐ and indefinite pronouns ☐ .

8 *Do you know **anyone who** has a van?* • *There must be **something (that)** we can do about the cold.*
9 *She insists that it's **you who** must apologize.* ~ *But it wasn't **I who** broke the window.*

We can also use the pronoun **those** (not **these**) with **who, that**, or reduced relative clauses.

10 ***Those who*** *know him well say he will fight.* • *Ask **those (who** are) waiting outside to come in.* •
   *His ideas are similar to **those (that)** we've heard before.* (NOT ~~similar to which~~) •
   *Organic vegetables are **those (that** have been) grown without the use of chemicals.*

We can use quantifiers as pronouns followed by **who** or **that** ☐ . We can also leave out the relative pronoun or use a reduced relative clause after quantifiers ☐ .

11 *We saw **some (that)** we liked in Italy.* • *I didn't find **a lot (that** was) written about Morrisseau.*
12 *There aren't **many who** like her.* • *There isn't **much that** he misses.*

B Add these clauses, with appropriate changes, to the sentences below.

his or her parents have passed away	they have completed their questionnaires
the wood of it is strong and durable	large flags were hanging from its upper windows
this person doesn't care about money	many of his paintings look like large comic strips

1 An orphan is a child ....

2 Have you ever met anyone .... ?

3 The oak is a kind of tree..

4 We passed an old palace ....

5 Those .... should hand them in.

6 Roy Lichtenstein, ..., helped establish pop art.

Prepositions in relative clauses

We can use prepositions at the beginning or the end of relative clauses. We usually put prepositions at the end in informal situations.

13 This is the room. I work <u>in it</u>. → *This is the room **in which** I work* OR *the room **that** I work **in**.*

When we put prepositions at the end, we usually use **that** (14) or no relative pronoun (15) at the beginning. In formal situations, we can include **which**, **who**, and **whom** at the beginning (16).

14 *Sneaks was the store **that** everybody went **to** for shoes.* • *There were bunk beds **that** we slept **in**.*

15 *Your opponent is the person _ you play **against**.* • *The day _ I'd been waiting **for** soon arrived.*

16 *Muskoka is the area **(which)** I grew up **in**.* • *Is he the boy **(whom)** you were telling us **about**?*

We always put the preposition at the end after a phrasal verb in a relative clause.

17 *There are things **(that)** he's had to cut back **on**.* (NOT … ~~things on that he's had to cut back.~~) • *He is a person **(whom)** I've always looked up **to**.* (NOT … ~~a person to whom I've looked up.~~)

When we put the preposition at the beginning of a relative clause, we use **which** (not **that**) (18) or **whom** (not **who**) (19).

18 *A clothesline is a wire **on which** clothes are hung to dry.* (NOT … ~~a wire on that clothes~~ …)

19 *A lot will be expected from people **to whom** a lot is given.* (NOT … ~~people to who a lot is given.~~)

There are some prepositions that we only use at the beginning (not the end) of relative clauses.

20 *The mid-nineteenth century was a period **during which** many people left Ireland.* (NOT … ~~a period which many people left Ireland during.~~)

Others used like this include **after**, **because of**, **before**, **below**, **besides**

C **Add these clauses, with appropriate changes, to the sentences below.**

you look through it	you must complete something before it
you look up to him or her	you can ask him or her where to find the books you need

1 A deadline is a point in time ....
2 A librarian is a person ....
3 A role model is a person ....
4 A telescope is a piece of equipment ....
   to see things that are far away.

D **Correct the mistakes in the use of relative clauses in this text.**

The saying for <s>that</s> ^which^ I had to find the meaning was, "People who live in glass houses shouldn't throw stones." My first guess was that it was about a situation which those want to fight should first think about defending themselves from attack. Obviously, a person who the house is made of glass, it's something is easily broken, should be careful. If you throw a stone, the person you threw the stone at him could throw it back and smash your house. However, this saying, the meaning of it I looked up in the *Oxford Dictionary of English Idioms*, is not really about fighting. It means that you should not criticize others for faults similar to you have yourself. I think this is good advice for anyone is critical of other people.

Relative clauses with **where, what, whatever,** etc.

Relative clauses with **where, when, why,** and **how**

We can use **where** instead of **in which, at which,** etc. after nouns for places (1) and after nouns such as **point** and **stage** (2). More figuratively, we can use **where** after nouns like **situation** (3).
  1 There's a small box. I keep keys <u>in it</u>. → *There's a small box **where/in which** I keep keys.*
  2 *We have reached a stage **where** we now have more people applying than we have space for.*
  3 *He prefers situations **where** strategy is more important than strength.*
Other nouns used like this include **activity, case, example, experience, society**

We can use **when** instead of **at which, during which,** etc. after nouns referring to time.
  4 *Do you have a moment **when** we can talk?* • *That was a period **when** everything was fine.*
We don't use **when** after **each / every time**: *That happens each / every time (that) it rains.*

After the noun **reason**, we can use **why** or no relative pronoun.
  5 *There may be good reasons **(why)** he couldn't come.* • *There's no reason **(why)** you can't do it.*

We can use **where, when, why,** and **how** in place of a noun and relative pronoun combined.
  6 *That's **where** his car was parked.* • *He pointed to **where** he used to live.* (= the place where) •
  *That's **when** I start.* • *They were talking about **when** they were children.* (= the time when) •
  *That's **why** I'm here!* • *She never told anyone **why** she had to leave.* (= the reason why) •
  *That's **how** it's done.* • *We showed him **how** we make rice pudding.* (= the way in which)
We don't use **how** after **the way**: *This is the way (that) we make it.* (NOT ~~the way how we make it.~~)

Relative clauses with **what**

We can use **what,** meaning "the thing(s) that," at the beginning of relative clauses used as objects (7) or subjects (8).
  7 She gave them <u>the things that</u> she had. → *She gave them **what** she had.*
  8 ***What** they're doing seems wrong.* (NOT ~~What they're doing it seems wrong.~~)

We don't use **what** after quantifiers (9) or after nouns or pronouns (10).
  9 *Some people lost **all (that)** they had invested.* (NOT ~~They lost all what they had invested.~~)
  10 *We'll buy **the food and everything (that)** we need later.* OR *We'll buy **what** we need later.*
  (NOT ~~the food what we need; everything what we need~~)

Relative clauses with **whatever, whoever,** etc.

We can use **whatever,** meaning "any thing(s) that" (11), and **whoever / whomever,** meaning "any person(s) that" (12), at the beginning of relative clauses used as objects or subjects. We use **whichever** when we're referring to "any thing(s) that" from a limited number or set of choices (13).
  11 *If you take the big boxes, I'll take **whatever** is left.* • ***Whatever** she did made them happy.*
  12 *We will work with **whomever** they send.* • ***Whoever** said those things is mistaken.*
  13 *Write in pen or pencil—**whichever** you prefer.* • *I'll go by bus or train—**whichever** is cheaper.*

We can use **whatever, whoever,** and **whichever** to say "it doesn't matter what, who, or which."
  14 *I'll always love you, **whatever** you do.* • *I'm not waiting all day for her, **whoever** she is.* •
  *He'll be in trouble, **whichever** he chooses.* • ***Whichever** way they go, we'll catch them.*

We can also use **wherever, whenever,** and **however** with the meanings "in or at any place, time, or way that ..." (15) and "it doesn't matter where, when, or how ..." (16).
  15 *He always keeps in touch, **wherever** he is.* • ***Whenever** I see Penny, she asks me about you.*
  16 *Please sit **wherever** you like.* • *Call **whenever** you can.* • *Just buy it, **however** much it costs.*

A Complete this email message with *how* (x2), *what, when, where,* and *why.*

Do you have a minute or two this morning (1) .... we can talk? I'm at a point
(2) .... I need to check with you about (3) .... I should organize the
report and (4) .... I should include or leave out. If you agree with (5) ....
I'm planning to organize it, then there's no reason (6) .... we can't have it finished
by Friday.

B Using a dictionary if necessary, complete the definitions with these words.

crime	prison	revenge
motive	quarantine	

that	when	which
what	where	why

1 .... is a place .... people are kept as punishment for crimes.
2 A .... is an explanation of .... someone acts in a particular way.
3 A .... is an offence for .... you may be punished by law.
4 .... is deliberate punishment or injury .... is inflicted in return for
.... someone has suffered.
5 .... is a period .... an animal or person is kept away from others in
order to prevent the possible spread of disease.

C Choose an ending (a–e) for each beginning (1–5) and add these words.

however, whatever, whenever, whichever, whoever

1 You can dress (...)   a .... they want to on Sunday morning.
2 We lived on potatoes (...) b .... we think would enjoy the party.
3 The girls can get up (...) c and .... else was available.
4 We'll go there (...)   d .... you want because it's really casual.
5 They said we could invite (...) e on Monday or Tuesday, ... day you're free.

D Complete the email with these words.

how, what, when, which, why, that, whatever, where, whichever

Thanks for your email and the good news about the report. I've tried several times to think about
the report, but then the phone rings and I have to pay attention to (1) .... is going
on right at that moment. I can assure you that this won't happen every time (2) ....
we have to do one of these quarterly reports, but right now I'm in a position (3) ....
every problem in the office seems to land on my desk, (4) .... is partly my own fault,
I know. Anyway, that's not (5) .... you wanted to hear about, I'm sure. I don't think
there's a slot in my schedule this morning (6) .... we can talk. How about late this
afternoon around three or four, (7) .... is best for you. If you already have some idea
(8) .... we should put the report together, then I agree with you that there shouldn't
be any reason (9) .... we can't complete it before the deadline. I'll talk to you later.

Mixed conditionals; order and punctuation in conditionals

Mixed zero and first (real) conditionals

In zero (or factual) conditionals, we usually use the same tense in both clauses (1), but we sometimes use a mixture of past and present tenses in the clauses (2).

1 *If it **snowed** heavily, we **didn't go** to school.* • *If she **works** late, I **wait** for her.*
2 *If you **saw** the movie, you **know** how it ends.* • *If they **don't understand** what to do, they probably **weren't listening** earlier.*

Some factual conditionals are used to describe habits in the past with **would** (**'d**). It has the same meaning as **used to**. It makes the sentence look like a hypothetical conditional, but it isn't.

3 *When we were kids, if it **rained** a lot, we**'d stay** indoors. But if it **was** sunny, we**'d** often **go** down to the lake.*

In first (or predictive) conditionals, we usually use the Simple Present in the **if**-clause (4), but we can also use the Simple Past (5) or Present Perfect (6) .

4 *If we **don't eat** now, we**'ll get** hungry later during the concert.*
5 *If you **studied** for the test, you **won't have** any problems.*
6 *If they**'ve finished** already, we**'ll give** them something else to do.*

When we use predictive conditionals to express a preference, we can include **would** with verbs of "liking" or "not liking" in the main clause (7). We can also use **would rather** plus the base form of a verb when we express a preference between alternatives that have been suggested (8).

7 *If it **isn't** too late, we**'d like** to watch the news on TV.*
8 *If it**'s** OK with you, I**'d rather stay** here.* (You suggested going somewhere else.)

Mixed second (unreal) conditionals

In second (or hypothetical) conditionals, instead of connecting an imaginary event to a possible present or future event using **would** (9), we can connect it to a possible past event with **would have** (10).

9 *If we **were** rich, we **would offer** to help those unfortunate people who are suffering.*
10 *If we **were** rich, we **would have offered** to help those unfortunate people who were suffering.*

In third (or counterfactual) conditionals, instead of connecting an imaginary past event to another past event using **would have** (11), we can connect it to a present event or situation using **would** (12).

11 *If your parents **hadn't met**, you **wouldn't have been born**.*
12 *If your parents **hadn't met**, you **wouldn't be sitting** here now.*

A **Add the following pronouns and the correct form of the verbs to the dialogue.**

she leave, you be, we need, I (not) wear

"If we want to make it to the theatre by 8:00, (1) .... to leave by 7:30," said Ivan.

    "I think Melinda has our tickets. If she does, (2) .... them for us at the ticket window."

    "Don't you want to wear something nicer?" asked Janice.

    "If I were you, (3) .... running shoes."

    "If you were me, (4) .... already .... on your way to the theatre."

Order and punctuation in conditionals

We can put the **if**-clause before or after the main clause (13). When we put the **if**-clause first, a sentence is clearer if you separate the two clauses with a comma (14).

   13 **If you feel dizzy,** you shouldn't go to work. • You shouldn't go to work **if you feel dizzy.**
   14 If I had some eggs, I could make a cake. ~ If I go and get some eggs, will you make one?

We can also emphasize the fact that the main clause is a consequence of the **if**-clause by putting **then** at the beginning of the main clause.

   15 The bus service is limited. If you rent a car, **then** you'll be able to go wherever you choose. •
      If the key isn't in the drawer, **then** Marta must have taken it.
Note that we don't use **so** in this way. (NOT ~~If it isn't there, so Marta must have taken it.~~)

When we add an **if**-clause after a main clause as an additional comment, we can use a comma to show that the **if**-clause is separate.

   16 I'd like to get a ticket, if they still have some. • Kate always goes to work, even if she feels bad.

B **Add the word *if* to the following description four times. Add the missing periods and commas.**

A number of idioms have come from the game of baseball someone is described as "batting a thousand" he or she is doing everything in a series of things right something is said to happen "right off the bat" it happens immediately and without delay someone "throws you a curveball" he or she surprises you often in an unpleasant way you "hit a grand slam" you have a sudden major victory.

C **Choose one verb from each pair to complete the clauses below. Add the completed clauses to the sentences (1–8), with appropriate punctuation.**

completes	don't watch	isn't	~~have paid~~	take
has completed	didn't watch	wasn't	are paying	took

didn't eat	will stay	would arrive	wouldn't be
hadn't eaten	would stay	would have arrived	wouldn't have been

▶ if you ..... have paid ..... the men already

  if Malik .... all her work already   if I .... so much at lunch

  if it .... going to be a problem   I .... so tired now

  if you .... television as a child   we .... in bed until noon

  if they .... the test earlier today   it .... by now, I'm sure

▶ ..If you have paid the men already,. they probably won't come back to work after lunch.
1 .... they won't get the results until tomorrow.
2 .... I'd like to leave my bike in the hallway tonight.
3 If Arvid sent the letter last week ....
4 If it was an extremely cold day outside ....
5 If the neighbour's dog hadn't started barking at 4 a.m. ....
6 I wouldn't feel so full now ....
7 .... we can let her leave early today.
8 .... you probably won't know why some of these people
  from old TV shows are famous.

Only if, even if, unless, whether, if so, etc.

Only if, if only

We use **only if** to emphasize a special condition (1). We sometimes put the word **only** before the verb in the main clause (2). The phrase **if and only if** is a more emphatic version, meaning "on one condition only" (3).

1. *These can be used **only if** there is an emergency.* • *He'll come **only if** he's ordered to.*
2. *My children will **only** eat a breakfast cereal **if** they've seen it on TV first.*
3. *You broke the law **if and only if** the agreement formed a legal contract.*

We can use **if only** in second (unreal) conditionals when we express wishes (4) or regrets (5).

4. ***If only** I had an extra copy, I'd gladly give it to you.* (I wish I had an extra copy.)
5. ***If only** she had been wearing a seat belt, she could have escaped without major injuries.*

Even if, even though

We use **even if** ("despite the possibility that") to say that a condition may exist, but it won't affect the future or possible situation described in the main clause (6). We use **even though** ("despite the fact that") to talk about the existence of a condition that won't affect the past or present situation in the main clause (7).

6. *We'll have a great time **even if** it rains.* (It may rain, but it won't stop us.) • ***Even if** Canadian History weren't a required subject, I'd enjoy learning about it.*
7. *We had a great time **even though** it rained.* (It rained, but it didn't stop us.) • ***Even though** Mathieu never studies, he passes all the tests.*

Unless

We use **unless** to say "except under the following circumstances" or "except if." It is used to draw attention to the condition as an exception and sometimes means the same as **if ... not**.

8. *He won't come **unless** you ask him.* (He won't come if you don't ask him.) • ***Unless** there's a miracle, I'll have to ask for extra time to complete my report.*

Unless is more limited than **if ... not**. We don't use **unless** in third (counterfactual) conditionals (9), when there is a negative cause or reason (10), or when we begin the main clause with **then** (11).

9. ***If** we had**n't** worked so hard, we would never have finished the project on time.*
10. ***If** he did**n't** have such a big nose, he'd be handsome.* (NOT ~~Unless he had such a big nose, ...~~)
11. ***If** they cannot agree on the terms of the contract, **then** a strike is inevitable.*

Whether (or not)

We can use **whether** instead of **if** when there are options (two or more possibilities) (12). We can use **whether or not** when one of the options is the negative of the other (13). We often put **or not** at the end of the clause, especially when we begin the sentence with **whether** (14).

12. ***Whether** we win or lose, we always enjoy playing.* • *I love soup, **whether** it's hot or cold.*
13. *They are going to send relief supplies **whether or not** the fighting has ended.*
14. ***Whether** it's raining **or not**, they're determined to play golf tomorrow.*

If so, if not, etc.

When we want to refer back to something that has already been mentioned, we can reduce the **if**-clause. There are several ways of doing this.

15. *Some books may have missing pages. **If so**, they can be exchanged.*
16. *Rules really must be enforced. **If not**, they can easily be ignored.* (If the rules aren't enforced ...)
17. *I think you should take the job. **If you do**, I'll help you get started.* (If you do take the job ...)

A Complete each sentence in such a way that it is as similar as possible in meaning to the sentence above it.

1 We'll have to leave without your friend if she doesn't come soon.
  Unless ....

2 We're going to start playing if Andy's ready or if he's not ready.
  Whether ....

3 If you aren't a registered student, they won't let you take books out of the library.
  They'll only ....

4 Our team played really well, but we didn't win the game.
  Even ....

B Complete each sentence with one of these words or phrases.

only if, unless, even though, if it isn't, if only, whether or not

1 The style of teaching at universities has hardly changed in the past 1000 years ....
  you count the invention of the blackboard 200 years ago.

2 Too many students leave the system thinking, "..................... I'd taken more practical courses."

3 Universities still rely on exams .... it is well-known that exams measure a very small
  part of a person's abilities.

4 Lectures are still the preferred teaching medium of professors .... they are of any real
  benefit to most students.

5 The system will change .... forces from the outside make it change.

6 .... a required course, then it has little chance of attracting high enrolment.

C We can mark a condition without using an *if*-clause. Using a dictionary if necessary, put
the conditional expressions from these sentences into one of the three categories below.

1 **Assuming** the information is correct, we have to reconsider our plans.

2 **Given** clear weather and good winds, the flight may arrive early.

3 **Providing (that) / Provided (that)** everyone is available, the next meeting will be on Monday.

4 Start slowly; **otherwise**, you won't be able to make it to the end.

5 **Suppose** your computer crashes—how will you get your files off it?

6 **Supposing** you won the lottery, what would you do?

7 You can keep playing your music **as long as / so long as** no one complains.

8 **What if** I sent the file by email—could you look at it before tomorrow's meeting?

9 **With** a little help, we could make this school a much better place.

10 **Without** your advice, I wouldn't have known how to do it.

A Simple condition ("if this is the case"): (1) Assuming, ...

B Exclusive condition ("**only if** this is the case"): ....

C Exceptional condition ("**if** this is **not** the case"): ....

Purpose clauses and result clauses

Purpose clauses with **so that**, **in order that**, **in order to**, etc.

We use purpose clauses to describe goals or the intended outcomes of actions. We can use **so that** (1) or **in order that** (2) to introduce purpose clauses, often with modals such as **can** (after a clause with a present tense verb) or **could** (after a past tense verb). We usually use **so** without **that** in informal situations (3).

    1 *I'm going early **so that I can find a good seat**. • I'll take my umbrella **so that I won't get wet**.*
    2 *Her father had worked hard for many years **in order that they could have a better life**.*
    3 *I'm going early **so I don't have to stand in a lineup**.* (NOT ~~in order I don't have to stand~~)

We often express purpose with a simple infinitive (**to clean**) (4). We also use the phrases **in order to** (5) or **in order not to** (6). Purpose clauses are sometimes used at the beginning of sentences (7).

    4 *Just use soap and water **to clean it**. • I think the boy fell when he was running **to catch the bus**.*
    5 *They recommend using bleach **in order to clean it thoroughly**. • You must fight **in order to win**.*
    6 *I'll clean the grill outside **in order not to make a mess in here**.* (NOT ~~in order to not make~~)
    7 ***In order to/To prevent vandalism,** all doors and windows must be locked securely.*

We sometimes form purpose clauses with **so as to** and **so as not to**.

    8 *It's designed that way **so as to** let in more light. • I'll put it near the door **so as not to** forget it.*

When we want to include a subject before the infinitive verb, we can begin a purpose clause with **in order for** and a noun phrase (9) or a pronoun (10).

    9 ***In order for the players to succeed,** they must work together.* (NOT ~~In order to succeed the players~~ ...)
    10 ***In order for you to win,** we will need to pray for a miracle.* (NOT ~~In order you to win~~ ...)

A Complete each sentence in such a way that is as similar as possible in meaning to the sentence(s) above it.

1 You should plan to leave early tomorrow. You'll avoid traffic jams on the way to the airport.
   In order to ....

2 We had to account for every cent we spent so that no money would be wasted.
   In order that ....

3 There must be a good source of light or plants won't grow indoors.
   In order for ....

4 We waited a few minutes until the rain stopped. We didn't want to get wet.
   So as ....

B Correct the mistakes in the use of conjunctions in these sentences.

1 Ms. Peters slipped quietly into the room at the back that nobody would notice her.

2 I don't like it when they spray those chemicals all over the place for kill insects.

3 In order to care people about another person, they must feel connected to that person.

4 I didn't say anything about Kevin's coming in late so as to not get him in trouble.

5 A stepladder is made of two parts joined at the top in order it can stand on its own.

6 We must keep our new designs secret in order not our competitors find and copy them.

Result clauses with **so, so … that, such … that**

We use result clauses beginning with **so** to describe effects or unintended outcomes. We put result clauses after main clauses (11), often separated by a comma (12).

11 *I'm tired **so I'm going to bed.*** • *He missed the bus this morning **so he was late for work again**.*

12 *There has been a reduction in the oil supply and increased demand**, so prices have risen**.*

In formal situations, **so that** is sometimes used instead of **so** to introduce a result clause. In a result clause, **so that** ("as a result") doesn't mean the same as **so that** ("in order that") in a purpose clause.

13 *A tree had fallen during the storm, **so that** the road was blocked and we couldn't go anywhere.* (NOT ~~in order that the road was blocked~~)

We can use an adjective (14), an adverb (15), or a quantifier (**few, little, many**, or **much**) (16) between **so** and **that** to form a result clause. We often leave out **that** in informal uses.

14 *It was **so nice (that) we ate lunch outside**.* • *The puppy was **so cute (that) she picked it up**.*

15 *The lecturer talked **so fast (that) none of us could understand him**.*

16 *There were **so many people (that) we had to wait**.* • *I ate **so much (that) I could hardly move**.*

We can also use a noun phrase (**nice weather**) between **such** and **that** to introduce a result clause (17). We often leave out **that** in informal situations, but not from certain fixed expressions (**in such a way that**) (18).

17 *It was **such nice weather (that) we ate lunch outside**.* • *I got **such a shock (that) I was speechless**.*

18 *Try to think about these problems **in such a way that you don't exaggerate their importance**.*

We can say, *It's so nice that …* or *It's such nice weather that …* (NOT ~~It's so nice weather that~~ …)

C Rewrite each pair of sentences as a single sentence, using **so** in a result clause.

1 They were feeling really tired. They went to bed early last night.

....

2 I wasn't able to do the homework. I forgot to take my textbook home with me.

....

3 Henrik is on a popular TV show. People recognize him when he's out shopping.

....

4 We had to drink bottled water. They said the tap water wasn't safe to drink.

....

D Add one of these clauses, changed to include **so … that** or **such … that**, to each of the following sentences.

That class was early	We had a wonderful time on vacation
The fire spread rapidly through their cabin	Wendy's children had bad colds this morning
~~The fog was thick~~	You and I don't have much money

▶ The fog was so thick (that) you couldn't see your hand in front of your face.

1 .... they couldn't save any of their belongings.

2 .... she couldn't let them go to school.

3 .... we can just throw it away carelessly.

4 .... we didn't want to come home.

5 .... everyone had trouble staying awake in it.

Contrast clauses and reduced adverbial clauses

Contrast clauses with **although, though, even though**, etc.

We use **although** ("despite the fact that") at the beginning of a clause that contains information that contrasts in an unexpected or surprising way with information in another clause.

> 1 (The sun was shining. I expected it to be warm.) ***Although the sun was shining,*** *it was cold.*
> (Josh is sick. I'd assume that he doesn't have to go to work.) *Josh has to go to work **although he's sick.***

We can also use **but** to express contrast, but not with **although**: *Josh is sick, but he has to go to work.* (NOT ~~Although Josh is sick, but he has to go to work.~~)

We often use **though** instead of **although** in informal situations (2). We can use **though** (not **although**) after adjectives or adverbs moved to the beginning of the clause (3).

> 2 ***Though Sabine's smart,*** *she isn't doing very well at school.* • *He has to go to work **though he's sick.***
> 3 ***Though*** *the test was **difficult,** we all passed.* → ***Difficult though*** *the test was, we all passed.*

In formal situations, **as** is also used in this structure: *Difficult as the test was, we all passed.*

When we want to emphasize a contrast, we can use **even though** when we are referring to past or present situations (4) and **even if** for future or possible situations (5). We don't use **even** with **although** or as a conjunction by itself.

> 4 *Aestus kept playing golf **even though it was raining.*** (NOT ... ~~even although it was raining.~~)
> 5 *Aestus would play golf **even if it were snowing.*** (NOT ... ~~even it were snowing.~~)

In formal situations, other conjunctions such as **whereas** (6) and **while** (7) are sometimes used to express a contrast between two clauses. The phrase **much as** is also used in contrast clauses with verbs such as **like, hate,** or **want** (8).

> 6 *Boys were encouraged to be adventurous **whereas girls were always told to stay clean.***
> 7 ***While no one doubts his ability,*** *his arrogant attitude has been difficult to accept.*
> 8 ***Much as I like music,*** *I can't listen to opera for long.* • ***Much as I want to,*** *I can't help you.*

We can use **despite the fact that** instead of **although** to introduce a contrast clause (9). We can also use the prepositions **despite** or **in spite of** plus gerunds instead of a clause with **although** (10).

> 9 ***Despite the fact that he had lots of friends,*** *he still felt really lonely sometimes.*
> 10 ***Despite studying hard,*** *I failed the test.* • *She wasn't satisfied **in spite of being paid extra.***
> (NOT ~~Despite I studied hard, I failed. She wasn't satisfied in spite of she was paid extra.~~)

A Complete each sentence in such a way that it is as similar as possible in meaning to the sentence above it.

1 I disagree with his point of view, but I understand why he thinks that way.
Although ....

2 Sotiris is still unemployed in spite of applying for about a dozen different jobs.
Though ....

3 While most people agreed that the car was a bargain, none of them wanted to buy it.
Even ....

4 Though it seems unlikely, the children may not want to go to the zoo on Saturday.
Unlikely ....

5 My grandparents didn't have very much money, but they were really generous.
Despite ....

Reduced adverbial clauses

An adverbial clause formed with a present participle is called a reduced adverbial clause (11). We put **not** before the present participle in the negative (12). Reduced adverbial clauses are also called participle clauses and are typically used in formal situations.

11 When he looked outside, he saw the police car. ➞ *Looking outside, he saw the police car.*

12 Because she didn't feel very well, she sat down. ➞ *Not feeling very well, she sat down.*

We can form reduced adverbial clauses with **having** + past participle for an earlier action, usually instead of a past perfect (13). We use **being** + past participle instead of a passive (14).

13 After he had retired, Cecil decided to travel. ➞ *Having retired, Cecil decided to travel.*

14 I was actually very flattered at first, because I was asked to work with one of the professors.
➞ *I was actually very flattered at first, being asked to work with one of the professors.*

We usually only use reduced adverbial clauses when the subjects of the main clause and the adverbial clause are the same (15). We avoid using reduced adverbial clauses when the subjects are different (16).

15 Because <u>it</u> was barking loudly, <u>the dog</u> scared us. ➞ *Barking loudly, the dog scared us.*

16 Because <u>it</u> was barking loudly, <u>we</u> were scared. (NOT ~~Barking loudly, we were scared.~~)

We can also form reduced adverbial clauses by using subordinating conjunctions such as **before** and **as if** with a present participle.

17 Before you leave, turn off all the lights. ➞ *Before leaving, turn off all the lights.*

18 He stood there, as if he was waiting for someone. ➞ *He stood there, as if waiting for someone.*
Note that **because** is not used in this way. (NOT ~~He stood there, because waiting for someone.~~)

When we use a subordinating conjunction such as **although**, **though**, **when**, or **while** with an adjective or a prepositional phrase (19), or with the past participle of a passive (20), we can leave out the subject + **be**.

19 *Although (they are) small, terriers are tough.* • *Adeel studied Greek while (he was) at McGill.*

20 *Though (it had been) broken, it still worked.* • *When (it is) seen from space, the earth is blue.*
The past participle is sometimes used without a conjunction: *Seen from space, the earth is blue.*

B **Add reduced versions of these adverbial clauses to the following sentences.**

although it manages	as if they were trying	until it makes sure	~~while they waited~~
although they were frustrated	once fares have been raised 25 cents		since it opened

▶ ..While waiting.. in line for buses during a recent subway delay, commuters displayed remarkable patience with their struggling transit system.

1 ...., most people just shrugged and went back to their newspapers, ... to ignore this latest inconvenience.

2 .... in 1954, the subway system has grown to serve the downtown and surrounding areas.

3 .... to make a substantial amount of money from fares, part of its operating costs come from the government.

4 The transit commission's argument is that, ..., service can expand far into the suburbs.

5 Many customers do not want the transit commission to increase fares again .... that the increased revenue will improve service.

Adding and contrasting connectors

Adding connectors: **also, as well, too**, etc.

When we want to show that we are adding information, we can use **also** in front (1) or mid position (2), but not usually in end position. We use **as well** or **too** in end position (3).

1 *You must not forget to include the postal code.* ***Also****, make sure you provide a return address.*
2 *Carl is good at French. He's* ***also*** *studying French cooking. I think he* ***also*** *speaks Italian.*
3 *He speaks a little Spanish* ***as well/too.*** (NOT ~~He speaks a little Spanish also.~~)

We can use other connectors, typically in front position, to show that we are adding to (4) or supporting (5) ideas presented earlier.

4 *We are sending food and water.* ***In addition****, they will need things like tents and blankets.*
5 *If you're ready, you should go ahead without me.* ***Besides****, I'd rather stay at home tonight.*
Others used formally include **furthermore, indeed, likewise, moreover, similarly**

We can use **in other words** (6) and **that is (to say)** (7) in front position when we want to show that information is being stated in another way.

6 *It's described as downsizing.* ***In other words****, people are losing their jobs.*
7 *He told me he wanted to join the army.* ***That is (to say)****, he wanted to wear a uniform and carry a gun.*

We can use connectors such as **in particular** (8), or **for example** and **for instance** (9), in front, mid, and end positions when we want to show that we are adding more-specific information.

8 *I enjoyed the book.* ***In particular****, I liked the details of life in Quebec as it used to be.*
9 *Shea doesn't help with the housework. He has,* ***for example****, never washed the dishes.* •
  This study of smoking habits is incomplete. There's no mention of teenagers, ***for instance****.*

Contrasting connectors: **however, instead**, etc.

We can use **however** and **instead** when we want to show that we are creating a contrast and introducing information which is unexpected or contradictory. We usually put **however** (10) and **instead** (11) in front position, but they can also be used in mid and end positions (12).

10 *She had hoped Jin would stay all weekend.* ***However****, he had to leave on Saturday.*
11 *He was supposed to stay here and help us move things.* ***Instead****, he went off to play baseball.*
12 *Extra security precautions had been proposed earlier. They were,* ***however****, considered too costly at the time. A tightening of existing security measures was undertaken* ***instead****.*
Others used formally include **in contrast, nevertheless, on the other hand, rather, yet**

Connectors used for adding or contrasting: **actually, in fact, after all**

We can use **actually** and **in fact** when we introduce information that adds something, often in support of a previous statement (13), or when the information contrasts with what was expected (14). We usually put both forms in front position, but they can also be used in end or mid position (15).

13 *I've known Kevin Rashad for years.* ***Actually****, we went to the same school.*
14 *Everyone thought the exam would be difficult.* ***In fact****, it turned out to be quite easy.*
15 *We went to the same school,* ***in fact****.* • *It* ***actually*** *turned out to be quite easy.*

We can use **after all** ("don't forget") in front or end position when we add information as a reminder (16). We can also use **after all** ("despite what was expected"), usually in end position, when we include information that contrasts with what was expected (17).

16 *I don't have to tell my parents everything.* ***After all****, I am over 18./I am an adult* ***after all****.*
17 *When I saw the rain, I didn't think we could go for a walk. Tony convinced me to go with him and we saw a beautiful rainbow. I'm so glad we decided to do it* ***after all****.*

A **Using a dictionary if necessary, add the following words and phrases to the definitions in this paragraph.**

facelift (×2), forklift, lift (×2), also (×2), for example, similarly, that is

An elevator, which is (1) .... known as a (2) .... in England, is a machine that you stand in to go up and down inside a building. The word *lift* is (3) ....
used for the action of taking someone somewhere in a car, described as "giving someone a (4) ...." Something very different is meant by a (5) ...., which is an operation to make someone look younger by, (6) ...., removing fat or pulling the skin tighter. (7) ...., the process of improving the appearance of the outside of a building can be described as "giving it a (8) ...." A (9) .... is a vehicle with special equipment, (10) ...., two long metal prongs sticking out in front, which is used for lifting and moving heavy things.

B **Add one group of connectors (not necessarily in this order) to each of the paragraphs.**

~~also~~ / however / in other words   indeed / in fact / too   actually / also / in particular

A Phil Cherneca was really in shape when he played rugby in school. He ^also^ stayed in good shape through university. Once he started working, things changed. He began eating a lot more and exercising a lot less. After a few years, his clothes were feeling tight and he was breathing really hard after running up stairs. He was out of shape.

B Phil didn't think he had time for outdoor activities, so he decided to join a gym. Like a lot more men these days, he started thinking about cosmetic surgery to improve his appearance. He wanted to get rid of some of the wrinkles around his eyes. Cosmetic surgeon Dr. Khalid Idris of Body Image in Toronto says, "Our clients used to be mostly women. Now we have more men than women coming in for certain types of surgery."

C The number of men seeking help from surgeons like Dr. Idris has increased dramatically in recent years. It's a trend that started in the US where cosmetic surgery is a $500 million business. The emphasis on looking young isn't limited to facelifts, but has created a huge demand for dental improvements and hair transplants.

C **Correct the mistakes in the use of connectors in these sentences.**

1 I'm still studying Canadian History. I'm hoping as well to take an Aboriginal History class.

2 I'd rather have chicken than fish if that's okay. I don't like actually fish very much.

3 I don't mind correcting students' homework. It's part of my job after all that.

4 I wouldn't say that Adam is the best student. In addition, he's certainly not the worst.

5 Recycling has been successful in schools. On the other hand, young children now automatically put their empty bottles in the recycling bin, not the garbage can.

Result, time, and listing connectors

Result connectors: **so, therefore**, etc.

We can use **so** in front position to show that what follows is a result of, or is caused by, earlier events (1). We sometimes use **therefore** when we want to emphasize a logical or necessary result (2). **Therefore** is more formal than **so**.

1 *We were moving some things out of the house when it started pouring rain.* **So** *everything got very wet.*
2 *The woman left the store with the necklace and she intended to do it.* **Therefore** *she is guilty of shoplifting.*

In formal situations, we can use **as a result**, usually in front position, to show that something is a direct result of earlier events.

3 *There has been an increase in population and a shortage of housing.* **As a result**, *rent has gone up and fewer students can afford to live within walking distance of the college.*

Others used formally include **accordingly, as a consequence, consequently, hence, thus**

Time connectors: **then, afterwards**, etc.

We can use **then** as a connector, usually in front position, to show that one action or situation is later than another (4) or follows logically from another (5). We sometimes use **then** at the beginning of a clause emphasizing what follows logically from a preceding **if**-clause (6).

4 *We had unpacked everything for the picnic and had just sat down.* **Then** *it started to rain.*
5 *Perhaps you could rent a car for a few days.* **Then** *you'd be able to go wherever you wanted.*
6 *If we allow the oil companies to succeed,* **then** *this area will be destroyed.*

We can use other connectors such as **afterwards** in front or end position when we're talking about the time relationship between one sentence and another.

7 *The movie was based on Cohen's first novel.* **Afterwards**, *the book became a bestseller.*

Others include **earlier, later, previously, subsequently**

We can use **meanwhile** ("during that time") to show that two things are happening during the same period of time (8). We can also use **meanwhile** ("before that time") to refer to something happening between two points in time (9). We usually put **meanwhile** in front position.

8 *My sister finished high school and got a good job.* **Meanwhile**, *I remained a poor student.*
9 *Let's meet again tomorrow.* **Meanwhile**, *I'll get in touch with Craig about your proposal.*

Others include **in the meantime** ("before that time"), **simultaneously** ("during the same time")

A Choose a sentence or clause (a–f) to follow each sentence or clause (1–6) and add *so* or *then*.

1 We got stuck in a bad traffic jam on the way to the concert. (...)
2 I know you don't like green peppers. (...)
3 If our operating budget is cut by 10 percent, (...)
4 It was a terrible morning, with a lot of problems in the office. (...)
5 A lot more people came to the meeting than they expected, (...)
6 The children have to do their homework every afternoon when they come home. (...)

a .... at lunchtime I spilled some tomato soup down the front of my white shirt.
b .... they can play or read a book.
c .... when we arrived, it had already started.
d .... we really will have to reduce services.
e .... I didn't put any in the salad.
f .... the room was very crowded.

Listing connectors

We can use **first** (or **firstly**), **second** (or **secondly**), etc. in front position to show the order of things in a list or a sequence. We sometimes use **then** or **next** instead of **second(ly)**, **third(ly)**, etc.

   10 *We really have to clean the house.* ***First***, *we have to take out the garbage.*
      Then/Second, *we'll have to wash all the dishes piled up in the kitchen sink.*
      Thirdly/Next *we really need to scrub the floor because it's so dirty.*

We can use **for starters** instead of **first(ly)** in front position to show that we are beginning a sequence of reasons to support or explain a preceding statement (11). We can use **finally** in front position to show that we are at the end of a list (12).

   11 *I hated working there.* ***For starters***, *everyone else was much older than me.*
Others include **first of all, in the first place, to begin with, to start with**

   12 ***Finally***, *I must thank my parents for their years of patience and support.*

We can use a phrase such as **to sum up** when we are going to provide a summary of points already made (13).

   13 ***To sum up***, *they liked our ideas, but they want to know more about the costs involved.*
Others include **in brief, in conclusion, in short, in summary, to conclude, to summarize**

B **Add these connectors to the following recipe.**

finally, first, second, then (×2)

To make fresh-cut fries for two, you'll need four large potatoes, an egg white, a quarter teaspoon of

cayenne pepper, and a pinch of salt. Slice each potato lengthwise, cut each slice lengthwise into long

sticks. Mix the egg white, cayenne, and salt in a bowl. Stir the potato sticks around in the mixture.

Spread the coated potato sticks on a greased baking sheet and bake them in the oven at 170° C

for 35 minutes.

C **Write one of these connectors or no connector (Ø), where appropriate, at the beginning of each of these sentences.**

as a result, ~~for starters~~, in short, secondly, so, then

▶ ....*Ø*........ Animal communication is different from human communication in two ways.
▶ *For starters,* Animal signals are always restricted to what is happening here and now.
1 .... When your dog comes to you and says, "Woof!," it always means, "I'm woofing now." It doesn't mean, "I woofed last night."
2 .... However, humans can easily talk about last night and things that happened years ago.
3 .... They can go on to talk about what they'll be doing tomorrow or next year.
4 .... Humans are also capable of talking about what doesn't even exist in plain sight.
5 .... They can refer to things like other universes without ever having seen them.
6 .... Animal communication consists of a fixed number of signals and each signal is used for one particular thing or occasion.
7 .... Human communication, on the other hand, is very creative and humans are able to invent new words, as illustrated by "woofing" in sentence 1.
8 .... Human communication has special properties not found in animal communication.

Focus structures

Fronting and inversion

We can focus attention on (or emphasize) one part of a sentence, such as the object, by moving it to front position. This is called fronting. We can use fronting, usually in formal situations, to link a sentence more closely to the preceding sentence (1) and to highlight a contrast (2).

1 She was coughing, sneezing and shivering. (He recognized these symptoms immediately.)
   → *These symptoms he recognized immediately.*
2 We met the Greens. (We liked Ms. Green, but we really didn't care for her husband.)
   → *Ms. Green we liked, but her husband we really didn't care for.*

After fronting, we often put the verb or auxiliary verb before the subject. This is called inversion. We usually use inversion with verbs describing place or movement after prepositional phrases (3) or after adverbs such as **here** and **there** (4) in front position.

3 I was told to sit on a chair in the middle of the room. (An old woman stood behind the chair.)
   → *Behind the chair **stood an old woman**. • Into the room **walked two men** wearing sunglasses.*
4 *Here **comes the bride**. • There **goes my bus**.* (NOT ~~There my bus goes.~~)

We also use inversion after negative words (**neither, nor**) (5), phrases beginning with **not** (6), and after adverbs such as **scarcely** or **seldom** (7) in front position.

5 *I don't like it. Neither **do my parents**. Nor **does anyone** else who I've asked.*
6 *Not until later **did we** notice the broken glass. • Not only **was the car** old, it had no windows.*
7 *Scarcely **had he** sat down when the phone rang. • Seldom **have I** heard such nonsense.*

We use inversion after **only** with prepositional phrases (8) or time expressions (9) in front position.

8 *I've looked for it in other places. Only in Italy **can you** find this special kind of ice cream.*
9 *Only after the test **will we** know if it worked. Only then **can we** decide what to do next.*

Inversion is also used after participles moved to front position, usually in narratives.

10 *The bedroom was empty. Lying on the bed **was a package**. Attached to it **was a small note**.*

A Complete the text by adding one of these expressions in each blank.

did she, is it, it was, she was, she would, was something, had she, it is, here comes, was she, would she, was part

Only occasionally (1) .... find herself reading someone else's newspaper, over his shoulder, as she sat waiting at the train station. Mostly (2) .... just not very interested, nor (3) .... willing to risk getting caught. Why (4) .... so embarrassing to get caught doing that, she wondered to herself. It isn't against the law or anything. But facing her today (5) .... that really caught her attention. One of our greatest fears in modern life, the headline said, was having to speak in public. The article offered ways to develop your confidence. Seldom (6) .... ever had to speak to an audience, but (7) .... her turn to give a 10-minute presentation in her French class that afternoon. Not only (8) .... have to speak to an audience, (9) .... have to do it in her second language. She felt the room getting hotter as she leaned forward to get a closer look. Suddenly blocking her view (10) .... of a large black beard and the big nose of the newspaper's owner. "Oops. Oh, (11) .... my train," she said quickly, as she stood up and stumbled toward the door. Public speaking isn't scary, she thought to herself; (12) .... public reading that makes me really nervous.

Cleft sentences

When we want to focus attention on (or emphasize) one part of a sentence, we can use special structures called cleft sentences. In a cleft ("divided") sentence, we divide the sentence into two parts and focus attention on one part. This part is usually stressed in speech. Some cleft sentences begin with **it** and are called **it**-clefts (11). Others begin with **what** and are called **wh**-clefts (12).

11 Martin + ate your pizza. → ***It was <u>Martin</u> who ate your pizza.***
    Martin ate + your pizza. → ***It was <u>your pizza</u> that Martin ate.***
12 Anna really likes + chocolate ice cream. → ***What Anna really likes is <u>chocolate ice cream</u>.***

It-clefts

We usually form **it**-clefts with **it** + **be** + an emphasized part + a relative clause beginning with **who** (13), **that** (14), or no relative pronoun (15).

13 Someone said Ali phoned earlier. (Ali didn't phone. Alex phoned.) → *No, it wasn't <u>Ali</u> who phoned. It was Alex.*
14 I'm not interested in anyone else. (I love you!) → *It's <u>you</u> that I love!*
15 Don't you like vegetables? ~ No, I like most of them. (I hate onions.) → *It's <u>onions</u> I hate.*

We usually use **it**-clefts when we want to focus attention on a noun or pronoun, but we can also focus on other parts of a sentence such as an adverb (16) or an adverbial clause (17).

16 You were supposed to be here yesterday. → *It was <u>yesterday</u> that you were supposed to be here.*
17 Things got worse after Jerusha left. → *It was <u>after Jerusha left</u> that things got worse.*

Wh-clefts

We usually form **wh**-clefts with a **what**-clause + **be** + an emphasized part. The emphasized part can be a noun phrase (18) or a noun clause (19).

18 I can't stop yawning. (I need a cup of coffee.) → *What I need is <u>a cup of coffee</u>.*
19 They don't know whether Richard's planning to stay here. (They're hoping that he'll leave soon.) → *What they're hoping is <u>that he'll leave soon</u>.*

We can also use **wh**-clefts to focus attention on verb phrases. We usually use a form of the verb **do** in the **what**-clause and the base form of the verb in the emphasized verb phrase (20). We sometimes use an infinitive in the emphasized verb phrase after **to do** in the **what**-clause (21).

20 Alison has an unusual job. (She repairs old clocks.) → *What she does is <u>repair old clocks</u>.*
21 Saj is ambitious. (He wants to study law.) → *What he wants to do is <u>(to) study law</u>.*

We sometimes use **all** ("the only thing") instead of **what** at the beginning.

22 I'll stop yawning soon. (I just need a cup of coffee.) → ***All I need is <u>a cup of coffee</u>.***

B **Complete each cleft sentence, emphasizing the underlined part, in such a way that it is as similar as possible in meaning to the sentence above it.**

1 <u>The cigarette smoke</u> is irritating my eyes.
   It ....

2 <u>We</u> had to clean up the mess.
   It ....

3 Carlos <u>watches TV in his room</u> instead of studying.
   What ....

4 Scientists now believe <u>that human activity is the cause</u>.
   What ....

Review test

There are four blanks in each of the following paragraphs.

Choose the best answer (**a**, **b**, **c**, **d**) for each blank.

1 It was (1) _____ late and I was beginning to (2) _____ tired, so I asked Rachel to finish her drawing and clean up. She held the drawing up for me to see. It (3) _____ a big black dog that (4) _____ sitting at a table.

1 a) becoming	b) being	c) getting	d) going
2 a) feel	b) feel as	c) feel it	d) feel to be
3 a) looked	b) looked as	c) looked for	d) looked like
4 a) seemed	b) seemed like	c) seemed to be	d) seemed was

2 The residents of Okanagan valley are (1) _____ only upset about some recent changes, but they're also very angry because (2) _____ consulted. Some families have lived and (3) _____ crops in the valley for many years, (4) _____ now their way of life is being threatened by developers who plan to build hundreds of new houses in the area.

1 a) both	b) either	c) neither	d) not
2 a) wasn't	b) weren't	c) it wasn't	d) they weren't
3 a) grew	b) grow	c) growing	d) grown
4 a) after	b) before	c) but	d) or

3 As soon as the war was over, the refugees (1) _____ to go back to the villages they (2) _____ about five years earlier. When they arrived, they (3) _____ that other groups from the east had moved into the ruined houses and (4) _____ rebuilding them.

1 a) have tried	b) had tried	c) tried	d) were tried
2 a) have left	b) had left	c) leave	d) were left
3 a) have found	b) had found	c) found	d) were found
4 a) are	b) have	c) had	d) were

4 Paul and Enrique meet in the corridor as Jack is locking his office door.

Paul: Oh, hello. I (1) _____ put this report in your mailbox, but perhaps you'd rather take it now.

Enrique: Oh, thanks. Actually, I (2) _____ have lunch right now, but if you put it in my mailbox, I (3) _____ it as soon as I (4) _____ back.

1 a) 'll	b) 'm going to	c) shall	d) was going to
2 a) 'll	b) 'm going to	c) shall	d) would
3 a) 'll be reading	b) 'll have read	c) 'll read	d) read
4 a) get	b) 'll be getting	c) 'll get	d) 'll have got

5 I'm not sure where Francine is. She (1) _____ have been waiting outside her house this morning so that we could give her a ride to work, but she wasn't there. Of course, she might (2) _____ sleeping and didn't hear us. If she had decided to take the bus, she (3) _____ arrived by now. I hope she isn't sick. (4) _____ I call her to see where she is?

1 a) may   b) must   c) ought   d) should
2 a) be   b) been   c) have   d) have been
3 a) will be   b) will have   c) would be   d) would have
4 a) Shall   b) Will   c) May   d) Ought

6 Don't you hate it when people say things like "Let's be careful, (1) _____ we?" It always sounds to me as if two of us (2) _____ to do something together, but in fact the other person (3) _____ doing anything. (4) _____ prefer it if they just said, "You should be careful," because that's what they really mean.

1 a) will   b) would   c) shall   d) should
2 a) are going   b) will   c) will be   d) would
3 a) won't   b) won't be   c) won't have   d) won't to
4 a) I'd   b) I'll   c) I'm   d) I've

7 Tommy, (1) _____ better slow down and wait for the rest of us. There are still lots of people on the platform, so the train (2) _____ come yet. You (3) _____ wait here while I buy our tickets. The ticket counter (4) _____ be over there where the lineup is.

1 a) you'd   b) you'll   c) you're   d) you've
2 a) can't   b) can't be   c) couldn't have   d) couldn't
3 a) ought   b) supposed to   c) should   d) should have
4 a) can   b) must   c) couldn't   d) can't

8 Joe has just returned to the computer lab where Andre works.
Joe: Who (1) _____ been using my computer?
Andre: I have (2) _____ idea. But these computers are for any student who wants to use them, (3)_____?
Joe: Of course. But (4) _____ you see me doing my work on that one before lunch? I hope it hasn't all been lost.

1 a) has   b) has he   c) have   d) have they
2 a) no   b) no longer   c) not   d) not an
3 a) aren't they   b) can't it   c) don't they   d) isn't it
4 a) aren't   b) didn't   c) don't   d) haven't

9 Liz is helping Adelfina clean out her apartment.
Liz: Did you want to keep all these old books or (1) _____?
Adelfina: I'm not sure. They look interesting, but (2) _____ of them would be worth anything.
Liz: So, (3) _____ of them do you think (4) _____ going to keep?

1 a) no   b) none   c) not   d) nothing
2 a) none   b) no one   c) not any   d) nothing
3 a) for what   b) for which   c) what   d) which
4 a) are   b) are you   c) you   d) you are

10 Last year we had (1) _____ more rain in the early spring and it made (2) _____ in the garden grow better. We probably had three or four (3) _____ strawberries as we're getting this year. I checked the strawberries in the garden this morning, but there (4) _____ that were ripe.

1 a) a large number of   b) a lot of   c) many   d) much
2 a) all   b) each   c) every   d) everything
3 a) time as many   b) time as much   c) times as many   d) times as much
4 a) was only a little   b) was only little   c) were only a few   d) were only few

11 I was sitting at my desk when there was a loud crash as something came flying through the window. At first I thought it was a rock, but then I realized it was a baseball. I picked up the ball and put it on the desk beside (1) _____. Two young boys appeared outside the broken window. They said they were sorry, but then they started arguing, with each blaming (2) _____ for causing the accident. Then suddenly one of them asked if (3) _____ could have the ball back. I said, "I don't think (4) _____. Not until you pay for this broken window." They looked at me, then at each other, and then they both started running.

1 a) me   b) mine   c) my   d) myself
2 a) another   b) one other   c) other   d) the other
3 a) it   b) then   c) they   d) Ø
4 a) it   b) so   c) that   d) Ø

12 Although they were described as (1) _____ ground-breaking, there isn't (2) _____ about the latest line of shoes from Santorelli. As one of the most famous designers (3) _____ Italy, Salvatore Santorelli is expected to do (4) _____ simply repeat the previous year's successful formula of "smart, but casual" sandals in a range of pastels.

1 a) complete   b) completely   c) little   d) a little
2 a) anything new very   b) anything very new   c) new anything very d) very new anything
3 a) by   b) in   c) of   d) to
4 a) as much as   b) more than   c) the best   d) the most

13 At a time when it has become so important (1) _____ in school, we shouldn't be (2) _____ to learn that more students are cheating than ever before. With so many of them anxious about (3) _____, students also now seem to believe that those who cheat are unlikely (4) _____.

1 a) succeed   b) succeeding   c) success   d) to succeed
2 a) surprise   b) surprised   c) surprises   d) surprising
3 a) fail   b) failed   c) failing   d) to fail
4 a) to catch   b) to be catching   c) to be caught   d) to have caught

14 There was one student who asked about (1) _____ it was okay to use a dictionary during the exam and I had to tell her (2) _____ it. Then she started arguing that she (3) _____ it was okay to use it in class. My response (4) _____ it was an exam, not a classroom exercise.

1 a) if   b) that   c) whether   d) why
2 a) don't use   b) no use   c) no using   d) not to use
3 a) think   b) was thinking   c) will think   d) thought
4 a) was that   b) that   c) is that   d) said that

15 The term "organic" can only be used to describe food (1) _____ in situations
   (2) _____ no artificial chemicals have been used. Anyone (3) _____ fertilizer
   (4) _____ containing chemicals to make tomatoes grow bigger, for example, is certainly
   not growing them organically.

   1 a) grown   b) that growing   c) where growing   d) which grown
   2 a) how   b) that   c) where   d) which
   3 a) use   b) used   c) uses   d) using
   4 a) what   b) when   c) which   d) Ø

16 (1) _____ in most other sports players are usually trying to get the most goals or points
   (2) _____ win, the opposite is true in golf. In a game of golf, it is the lowest score that wins.
   Each player must try to get his or her ball in the hole (3) _____ as few shots as possible.
   For each hole there is a given number of shots called "par." When a player uses one shot less than par,
   it's called a "birdie," and (4) _____ get an "eagle" a player must use two shots less than par.

   1 a) Even although   b) In spite of   c) Instead of   d) Whereas
   2 a) for   b) in order to   c) so that   d) such that
   3 a) use   b) uses   c) used   d) using
   4 a) so as to   b) such that   c) in order to   d) so that

17 What the recent use of DNA testing has shown (1) _____ eyewitness testimony may not
   always be reliable. (2) _____, an eyewitness testified that he saw Gilbert Medeiros with
   Angela Anderson shortly before the young woman was murdered and, (3) _____ that
   testimony, Medeiros was convicted and sent to prison. Not until much later (4) _____
   discovered through DNA testing that someone other than Medeiros had been responsible
   for Anderson's death.

   1 a) is it   b) is that   c) it is   d) that is
   2 a) For example   b) In addition   c) On the other hand d) Therefore
   3 a) afterwards   b) as a consequence c) as a result of   d) subsequently
   4 a) it was   b) they   c) was   d) was it

18 Do you sometimes feel anxious or irritable when you're driving? It may be the smell inside your car
   (1) _____ is determining how you feel. A recent study of Canadian drivers found that the
   smell of peppermint or cinnamon improved their performance by reducing anxiety more than
   20 percent. Alertness (2) _____ increased by almost 30 percent. (3) _____,
   the smell of cake or fast food made drivers more irritable and caused them to speed, probably
   because those smells, (4) _____, stimulate hunger and make drivers more anxious to
   get where they're going sooner.

   1 a) it   b) that   c) what   d) which
   2 a) also   b) as well   c) besides   d) moreover
   3 a) In conclusion   b) In contrast   c) In other words   d) In particular
   4 a) in fact   b) however   c) besides   d) also

Appendix: Regular and irregular verbs

Regular verbs

We add **-ed** (1) or simply **-d** (2) to the base form of regular verbs to make the Simple Past and past participle forms.

    1 *I ask**ed** him, but he hasn't answer**ed** yet.* • *We want**ed** to know.* • *I have wait**ed** patiently.*

    2 *They agre**ed** that it was a good idea.* • *That's why we have continu**ed**.* • *She hasn't smil**ed** much.*

Before adding **-ed** to some verbs, we double the final consonant (after a single written vowel, in stressed syllables).

    3 *She had pla**nn**ed to visit us and regre**tt**ed that poor health had sto**pp**ed her.*

Others include **dragged, occurred, permitted, preferred, ripped, robbed, slipped, trimmed**

We change the final **-y** (after a consonant) to **-i-** before **-ed** in some verbs.

    4 *Have you tr**i**ed to get a scholarship? ~ I appl**i**ed for one, but they haven't repl**i**ed yet.*

Others include **carried, copied, cried, hurried, identified, implied, studied, testified, worried**

Irregular verbs

We use special forms for the Simple Past of some verbs.

    5 *We **saw** Riyaad Ali yesterday.* • *I **forgot** I had your keys.* • *They **understood** what I **taught** them.*

We add **-en** (6) or **-n** (7) to the base form of some verbs to make the past participle.

    6 *Where have you be**en**?* • *Have you eat**en** anything?* • *I had hidd**en** it, but it had fall**en** out.*

    7 *I haven't see**n** that movie.* • *Have you know**n** him a long time?* • *They've drive**n** up from Moose Jaw.*

We use the base form of some verbs for the Simple Past and past participle.

    8 *Yesterday I **hit** my forehead on the shelf and **cut** it, but it hasn't **hurt** too badly today.*

Others include **bet, burst, cost, forecast, let, put, quit, ride, set, shut, split, spread, thrust**

Some verbs are used with both regular and irregular forms.

    9 *Who <u>burned</u> / burnt the toast?* • *I dreamed / <u>dreamt</u> about you.* • *He <u>spilled</u> / spilt some milk.*

Others include **kneeled / <u>knelt</u>, leaped / <u>leapt</u>, learned / learnt, lighted / <u>lit</u>, speeded / <u>sped</u>**

Note that the underlined form of each verb is currently more common in Canadian English.

Common irregular verbs

BASIC FORM	SIMPLE PAST	PAST PARTICIPLE
be	was, were	been
become	became	become
begin	began	begun
bend	bent	bent
bet	bet	bet
bite	bit	bitten
blow	blew	blown
break	broke	broken
bring	brought	brought
build	built	built
burst	burst	burst
buy	bought	bought
catch	caught	caught
choose	chose	chosen
come	came	came
cost	cost	cost
cut	cut	cut
dig	dug	dug
do	did	done
draw	drew	drawn
drink	drank	drunk
drive	drove	driven
eat	ate	eaten
fall	fell	fallen
feed	fed	fed
feel	felt	felt
fight	fought	fought
find	found	found
fly	flew	flown
forget	forgot	forgotten
forgive	forgave	forgiven
freeze	froze	frozen
get	got	got
give	gave	given
go	went	gone
grow	grew	grown
have	had	had
hear	heard	heard
hide	hid	hidden
hit	hit	hit
hold	held	held
keep	kept	kept
kneel	knelt	knelt
know	knew	known
lay	laid	laid
lead	led	led
leave	left	left
lend	lent	lent
let	let	let
lie	lay	lain

BASIC FORM	SIMPLE PAST	PAST PARTICIPLE
light	lit	lit
lose	lost	lost
make	made	made
mean	meant	meant
meet	met	met
pay	paid	paid
put	put	put
read	read	read
ride	rode	ridden
ring	rang	rung
rise	rose	risen
run	ran	run
say	said	said
see	saw	seen
sell	sold	sold
send	sent	sent
set	set	set
shake	shook	shaken
shine	shone	shone
shoot	shot	shot
show	showed	shown
shut	shut	shut
sing	sang	sung
sink	sank	sunk
sit	sat	sat
sleep	slept	slept
slide	slid	slid
speak	spoke	spoken
spend	spent	spent
spit	spat	spat
split	split	split
spread	spread	spread
stand	stood	stood
steal	stole	stolen
stick	stuck	stuck
strike	struck	struck
swear	swore	sworn
sweep	swept	swept
swim	swam	swum
take	took	taken
teach	taught	taught
tear	tore	torn
tell	told	told
think	thought	thought
throw	threw	thrown
understand	understood	understood
wake	woke	woken
wear	wore	worn
win	won	won
write	wrote	written

Glossary

This is a list of grammar terms with explanations of what they mean. Words printed in CAPITALS in the explanations are themselves grammar terms and can be found in their own place in the glossary.

action verb: a VERB used to describe what we do or what happens (*I **ate** lunch.*); compare STATIVE VERB

active verb: a VERB form used to describe what the SUBJECT does (*A thief **stole** my car.*); compare PASSIVE

adjective: a word such as **new** or **good-looking** used to modify a NOUN (*Katia's **new** boyfriend is **good-looking**.*)

adverb: a word such as **really** or **recently** used to modify a VERB, ADJECTIVE, ADVERB, or SENTENCE (*I met him **recently** and he's **really** good-looking.*)

adverbial: an ADVERB (**later**), PREPOSITIONAL PHRASE (**in town**), or ADVERBIAL CLAUSE (**after I finish work**) used to provide additional information in a CLAUSE or a sentence (*I'll meet you **in town** later **after I've finished work**.*)

adverbial clause: a CLAUSE typically introduced by a SUBORDINATING CONJUNCTION such as **because** and providing information such as when or why something happens (*I can't go out **because I have to study**.*)

agent: the person or thing that does or causes an action, typically the SUBJECT in ACTIVE sentences (***Patrick deWitt** wrote The Sisters Brothers.*)

article: a word used as a DETERMINER before a NOUN, either as a DEFINITE ARTICLE (**the**) or an INDEFINITE ARTICLE (**a/an**) (***The** car had **a** flat tire.*)

attributive adjective: an ADJECTIVE used before a NOUN (*She had **red** hair and **green** eyes.*); compare PREDICATIVE ADJECTIVE

auxiliary verb: a form of **be, do, have**, or a MODAL used with a MAIN VERB to form different TENSES, negatives, and QUESTIONS (***Have** you eaten yet?*)

bare infinitive = base form

base form: the form of a VERB such as **be** or **eat**, as listed in a dictionary

clause: a group of words including a SUBJECT and a VERB that forms a SIMPLE SENTENCE (*She left yesterday.*) or is part of a COMPLEX SENTENCE (*She left before you came.*) or COMPOUND SENTENCE (*She left and I'm glad.*)

cleft sentence: a structure in which a sentence (*I'm not supposed to drink coffee.*) is divided into two parts and attention is focused on one part, using an IT-CLEFT (*It's coffee that I'm not supposed to drink.*) or a WH-CLEFT (*What I'm not supposed to drink is coffee.*)

collective noun = group noun

common noun: a NOUN that is not the name of anyone or anything (*The **car** had a flat **tire**.*); compare PROPER NOUN

comparative: an ADJECTIVE or ADVERB with **-er** (**healthier**) or **more/less** (**less expensive**), often followed by **than**, used to say that something has more or less of a quality than another (*Fish is **healthier** and **less expensive** than meat.*); compare SUPERLATIVE

complement: a word or phrase used after a LINKING VERB, typically describing the SUBJECT (*She is **a student** so she isn't **rich**.*)

complex preposition: a PREPOSITION that consists of two or more words (*In addition to me, there were three other people waiting in front of the entrance.*); compare SIMPLE PREPOSITION

complex sentence: a sentence with two or more CLAUSES joined by a SUBORDINATING CONJUNCTION such as **because, before**, etc. (*I went to bed because I was tired.*); compare COMPOUND SENTENCE

compound adjective: an ADJECTIVE that consists of two words joined by a hyphen (*a good-looking person, a home-cooked meal*)

compound-complex sentence: a sentence with three or more CLAUSES joined by both a COORDINATING CONJUNCTION and a SUBORDINATING CONJUNCTION (*Dave read a magazine and I went to bed because I was tired.*); compare COMPLEX SENTENCE and COMPOUND SENTENCE

compound noun: two or more words used together as a NOUN to refer to a person or thing (*a bus driver, an application form*)

compound sentence: a sentence with two or more CLAUSES joined by a COORDINATING CONJUNCTION (**and, but**, or **or**) (*Dave read a magazine and I went to bed.*); compare COMPLEX SENTENCE

conditional: a structure in which one CLAUSE, typically beginning with **if**, is presented as a condition for something in another clause (*If I have time, I'll help you.*)

conjunction: a word such as **and, but**, or **or** that links words, phrases, or sentences (*It's late and I want to go home.*)

connector: a word (**however**) or phrase (**in addition**) typically used to link sentences and sometimes CLAUSES (*They didn't win. However, they played better than they did last week. In addition, they scored two goals.*)

continuous = progressive

contracted form: a short form of a word (**I've, he's, she'd, we'll, they won't**)

coordinating conjunction: **and, but, or** (*I'll write or I'll call you.*); compare SUBORDINATING CONJUNCTION

countable noun: a NOUN that can be singular (**book, child**) or plural (**books, children**) and used to refer to people or things as separate individuals; compare UNCOUNTABLE NOUN

counterfactual conditional = third conditional

defining relative clause: a RELATIVE CLAUSE used to identify or classify people or things (*Do you know the man who lives upstairs?*); compare NON-DEFINING RELATIVE CLAUSE

definite article: **the** (*Can you see the moon?*); compare INDEFINITE ARTICLE

demonstrative: one of the words **this, that, these,** or **those** used as a DETERMINER before a NOUN (*this book*) or as a PRONOUN instead of a NOUN PHRASE (*I don't like that.*)

demonstrative pronoun: one of the words **this, that, these,** or **those** used instead of a NOUN PHRASE (*I like these better than those.*)

determiner: a word used before a NOUN such as an ARTICLE (**a/an, the**), a DEMONSTRATIVE (**this, that, these, those**), or a POSSESSIVE (**my, your, his, her, its, our, their**) (*A friend sent me this funny card for my birthday.*)

direct object: a word or phrase identifying the one(s) affected by the action of the verb (*I dropped the ball.*); compare INDIRECT OBJECT

direct speech: the original words of a speaker, usually presented in QUOTATION MARKS, in a report of what was said (*He said, "I'm tired."*); compare INDIRECT SPEECH

ellipsis: the practice of leaving out words or phrases instead of repeating them (*Raj came in and __ sat down.*)

empty object *it*: the word **it** in DIRECT OBJECT position, not used to refer to anything (*I hate it when I miss the bus.*)

empty subject *it*: the word **it** in SUBJECT position, not used to refer to anything (*It was nice to go for a walk even though it was raining.*)

empty subject *there*: the word **there** in SUBJECT position, not used to refer to anything (*There isn't any food left.*)

equative: an ADJECTIVE or ADVERB in the structure (**not**) **as ... as**, used to describe something as similar (or not) to another in some way (*Your cat is as big as my dog.*)

factual conditional = zero conditional

first conditional: a type of REAL CONDITIONAL used to express a fixed connection between two events now, in the past, or always (*If the fruit is soft, it's ready to eat.*)

focus structure: a structure such as FRONTING or a CLEFT SENTENCE used to focus attention on one part of a sentence (*Tea I can drink. It's coffee I'm not supposed to drink.*)

fraction: a word or phrase such as **half** or **two-thirds** used as a QUANTIFIER with **of** before a DETERMINER or PRONOUN to describe a part of something (*Two-thirds of the students are from Japan.*)

fronting: a structure in which one part of a sentence (*I can't drink coffee*) is moved to front position (*Coffee I can't drink because it gives me a headache.*)

generic noun: a NOUN used in making a general statement about something, not about a specific example (*Women live longer than men.*)

generic pronoun: a PRONOUN such as **one, they, we,** or **you** used with the meaning "people in general" (*They say you can't teach an old dog new tricks.*)

gerund: a word with the same form as the PRESENT PARTICIPLE, but used as a NOUN (*I enjoy walking.*)

group noun: a NOUN such as **committee** or **team** used to refer to a group of people as a single unit (*The committee chooses the national team.*)

hypothetical conditional = second conditional

imperative: the BASE FORM of the VERB, typically used to give orders (*Stop!*)

indefinite adverb: an ADVERB such as **anywhere** or **everywhere** used to describe places in a very general way (*I've looked everywhere, but I can't find my notebook anywhere.*)

indefinite article: **a/an** (*Would you like an apple or a banana?*); compare DEFINITE ARTICLE

indefinite pronoun: a PRONOUN such as **someone** or **anything** used to describe people and things in a very general way (*Someone called earlier, but he or she didn't say anything.*)

indirect object: a word or phrase used after a VERB such as **give** or **send**, identifying the person or thing receiving something (*I gave Bob some money. I sent a letter to them.*); compare DIRECT OBJECT

indirect question: a version of a previously asked QUESTION, not the exact words, presented in a NOUN CLAUSE as a report of a WH-QUESTION (*He asked **what we were doing.***) or a YES/NO QUESTION (*He asked **if we were from Sweden.***)

indirect speech: a version of a previous utterance, not the exact words, presented in a NOUN CLAUSE as a report of what was said (*He said **that he was tired.***); compare DIRECT SPEECH

infinitive: to plus the BASE FORM of a VERB (*I'm hoping **to win.***)

-ing form = gerund

intransitive verb: a VERB that never has an OBJECT (*I can't **sleep.***); compare TRANSITIVE VERB

inversion: a structure in which a VERB or AUXILIARY VERB is put before the SUBJECT (*Into the room walked two men.*)

***it*-cleft:** a structure in which a sentence (*I'm not supposed to drink coffee.*) is divided into two parts, the first part with **it** + **be** + an emphasized element and the second part a RELATIVE CLAUSE (*It's coffee (that) I'm not supposed to drink.*); compare WH-CLEFT

linking verb: a VERB such as **be, become,** or **seem,** used with a complement, typically describing the SUBJECT (*She **is/seems** unhappy.*)

linking word = connector

main verb: the VERB in a CLAUSE (*Did you **follow** that? I **understood** what she **said.***); compare AUXILIARY VERB

mass noun = uncountable noun

mixed conditional: a type of CONDITIONAL in which there is an unusual combination of TENSES in the two CLAUSES (*If you saw the movie, you'll remember the battle scene.*)

modal: an AUXILIARY VERB such as **can, could,** or **must,** used with the BASE FORM of a VERB to describe what is possible, permitted, necessary, etc. (*You **must** leave now.*); compare PHRASAL MODAL

multiplier: a word or phrase such as **twice** or **five times** used as a QUANTIFIER before a DETERMINER to describe how often or how much more something is (*They pray **five times** a day.*)

negative: a sentence or CLAUSE with an AUXILIARY VERB plus **not** or **-n't** and a MAIN VERB (*I **don't** care.*)

negative adverb: a word or phrase such as **never** or **no longer** used as an ADVERB (*He **never** studies.*)

nominal clause = noun clause

non-count noun = uncountable noun

non-defining relative clause: a RELATIVE CLAUSE used to provide extra information, typically set off by commas (*My friend Pedro, **who lives upstairs**, has a cat.*); compare DEFINING RELATIVE CLAUSE

non-finite form = base form

noun: a word used for someone or something, either as a COMMON NOUN (**book, courage**) or a PROPER NOUN (**Suzuki, Haida Gwaii**)

noun clause: a THAT-CLAUSE (*I know **that it's late.***) or a WH-CLAUSE (*I didn't know **what you were doing.***) used like a NOUN PHRASE

noun phrase: a phrase in which the main word is a NOUN and which is used as a SUBJECT or an OBJECT (***Their new condo** is really big so they're having **a party** for **sixty people** on **Saturday night.***)

object: a NOUN, NOUN PHRASE, or PRONOUN used as a DIRECT OBJECT (*He took **the money**.*), INDIRECT OBJECT (*I gave **him** the money.*), or after a PREPOSITION (*He took it with **him**.*)

object pronoun: a PERSONAL PRONOUN (**me, you, him, her, it, us, them**) used as an OBJECT (*James gave **them** to **me**, not **her**.*)

pair noun: a NOUN used for something made of two matching parts such as **scissors** or **pants**.

parenthetical noun clause: a NOUN CLAUSE used after a NOUN to provide extra information, typically set off by commas, dashes, or parentheses (*His first suggestion, **that we should go to Red Deer**, wasn't very popular.*)

participle: a VERB form, either the PRESENT PARTICIPLE (**breaking, repairing**) or the PAST PARTICIPLE (**broken, repaired**)

participle adjective: an ADJECTIVE derived from a PRESENT PARTICIPLE (**surprising**) or a PAST PARTICIPLE (**shocked**) (*She seemed **shocked** by the **surprising** news.*)

participle clause = reduced adverbial clause

particle: a PREPOSITION (**on**) or ADVERB (**away**) combined with a VERB to make a PHRASAL VERB (*He put **on** his jacket and walked **away**.*)

passive: a VERB form with **be** plus the PAST PARTICIPLE of a TRANSITIVE VERB, used to describe what happens to the SUBJECT (*My car **was stolen**.*); compare ACTIVE

past participle: a VERB form such as **broken** or **repaired**, used in the PERFECT (*I had **broken** my watch.*) and the PASSIVE (*It was **repaired**.*)

Past Perfect: a VERB form using **had** + PAST PARTICIPLE (***Had** you **forgotten** anything?*)

Past Progressive: a VERB form using **was** or **were** + PRESENT PARTICIPLE (*The baby **was sleeping**.*)

percentage: a phrase such as **ten percent** (**10%**) used as a QUANTIFIER with **of** before a DETERMINER or PRONOUN to describe a part of something (***Ten percent** of the population is living in poverty.*)

perfect: a VERB form using **have** + PAST PARTICIPLE (***Have** you **forgotten** anything?*)

personal pronoun: one of the SUBJECT PRONOUNS (**I, you, he, she, it, we, they**) or OBJECT PRONOUNS (**me, you, him, her, it, us, them**)

personification: the treatment of an abstract idea or a thing as if it was a person (***Death's** cold hand touched his shoulder.*)

phrasal modal: a phrase such **as be able to, be going to**, or **have to**, used instead of a MODAL (*We **have to** wait for Cathy.*); compare MODAL

phrasal verb: a VERB + PARTICLE combination such as **sleep in** or **put on** (*He **put on** his shoes.*)

Pluperfect = Past Perfect

possessive: a word such as **my, your**, or **their** used as a DETERMINER before a NOUN (**my chair, your money**) and **mine, yours**, or **theirs** used as a PRONOUN instead of a NOUN PHRASE (*I found **mine**, but I couldn't find **yours**.*)

possessive determiner: **my, your, his, her, its, our, their**; compare POSSESSIVE PRONOUN

possessive noun: a NOUN plus an apostrophe with **s** (**Lee's car**) or without s (**The Weakerthans' first CD**)

possessive pronoun: mine, yours, his, hers, ours, theirs; compare POSSESSIVE DETERMINER

predicative adjective: an ADJECTIVE used after a LINKING VERB (*Her hair was **red** and her eyes were **green**.*); compare ATTRIBUTIVE ADJECTIVE

predictive conditional = first conditional

preposition: a word such as **at** or **on**, or a phrase such as **in front of**, used before a NOUN, NOUN PHRASE, or PRONOUN in a PREPOSITIONAL PHRASE (*I'll meet you **at** noon **on** Friday **in front of** the library.*)

prepositional phrase: a PREPOSITION plus a NOUN, NOUN PHRASE, or PRONOUN (**on the table, in front of me**)

present participle: a VERB form such as **sleeping**, used in the PROGRESSIVE (*Is he **sleeping**?*); compare **past participle**

Present Perfect: a VERB form using **has** or **have** + PAST PARTICIPLE (***Have** you **forgotten** anything?*)

Present Progressive: a VERB form using **am, is,** or **are** + PRESENT PARTICIPLE (*The baby **is sleeping**.*)

progressive: a VERB form using **be** + PRESENT PARTICIPLE (*The baby **is sleeping**.*)

pronoun: a word such as **she, anything,** or **herself** used instead of a NOUN or NOUN PHRASE (*Jaunita is very old and **she** can't do **anything** by **herself**.*)

proper noun: a NOUN with a capital letter used as the name of someone or something (***Elsa** is from **Switzerland**.*); compare COMMON NOUN

quantifier: a word such as **many** and **some** or a phrase such as **a few** and **a lot** (**of**) used to refer to quantities (***Some** people have **a lot of** money.*)

question: a sentence with an AUXILIARY VERB before the SUBJECT and MAIN VERB, used as a WH-QUESTION (*When did he leave?*) or a YES/NO QUESTION (*Did he leave?*)

question tag: an AUXILIARY VERB plus a SUBJECT PRONOUN used as a short form of a QUESTION added after a statement (*He hasn't left yet, **has he**? He's still here, **isn't he**?*)

quotation marks: a pair of marks ("...") inside which we put DIRECT SPEECH, special words or phrases, and some titles (*"I'm tired," he said.*) (*Have you read "In Flanders Fields"?*)

real conditional: a type of CONDITIONAL in which the events happen, have happened, or are likely to happen (*If I open the door, the cat will run out.*); compare UNREAL CONDITIONAL

reciprocal pronoun: **each other** and **one another**, used when an action or feeling goes both ways between people or things (*My brothers avoid **each other** whenever possible.*)

reduced adverbial clause: an ADVERBIAL CLAUSE formed with a PARTICIPLE or a SUBORDINATING CONJUNCTION plus a PARTICIPLE (**(Before) leaving the house**, he turned off the lights.*)

reduced negative: a short form of a NEGATIVE, typically formed with a CONJUNCTION plus **not** (*Do you want this **or not**? **If not**, can I have it?*)

reduced relative clause: a RELATIVE CLAUSE formed with a PARTICIPLE and no RELATIVE PRONOUN (*I saw some people **waiting** outside.*)

reflexive pronoun: **myself, yourself, himself, herself, itself, ourselves, yourselves,** and **themselves,** used when the OBJECT of the VERB is the same person or thing as the SUBJECT of the verb (***He** burned **himself** cooking dinner.*)

relative clause: a CLAUSE typically introduced by a RELATIVE PRONOUN and used to provide additional information about a NOUN PHRASE in a preceding CLAUSE (*I was on a bus **that was packed with children who were making a lot of noise.***)

relative pronoun: the words **who, whom, which,** and **that** used to introduce a RELATIVE CLAUSE (*I have a friend **who** can fix computers.*)

reported speech = indirect speech

reporting verb: a VERB such as **say** or **reply** used with DIRECT SPEECH (*He **said,** "Hello."*) or INDIRECT SPEECH (*I **replied** that I was busy.*)

rhetorical question: a sentence in the form of a QUESTION used to make a statement. (*Who cares?*)

second conditional: a type of UNREAL CONDITIONAL used to express a distant and unlikely connection between one imaginary event and another (*If I had a lot of money, I'd buy a Mercedes.*)

simple preposition: a PREPOSITION that is a single word such as **at, during, in,** or **without**; compare COMPLEX PREPOSITION

simple sentence: a single CLAUSE with a SUBJECT and a VERB (*Mary sneezed.*), which may also include an OBJECT and an ADVERBIAL (*We ate lunch in a café.*); compare COMPOUND SENTENCE and COMPLEX SENTENCE

split infinitive: an INFINITIVE with an ADVERB between **to** and the VERB (*I want **to really understand** him.*)

stative verb: a VERB used to describe a state, not an action (*I **know** that he **has** a lot of money.*); compare ACTION VERB

subject: a NOUN, NOUN PHRASE, or PRONOUN typically used before a VERB to identify who or what performs the action of the VERB (***Tony** lost his keys and **I** found them.*)

subject pronoun: a PERSONAL PRONOUN (**I, you, he, she, it, we, they**) used as SUBJECT (***He** wants to get married and **she** doesn't.*)

subject-verb agreement: the relationship of a singular SUBJECT with a singular VERB (***He is** eating lunch.*) or a plural SUBJECT with a plural verb (***They are** eating lunch.*)

subjunctive: a special use of the BASE FORM of a VERB in a NOUN CLAUSE, sometimes called the present subjunctive (*They have proposed that taxes **be** increased.*); also the use of **were** in a NOUN CLAUSE after the VERB **wish** (*I wish I **were** older.*) and in a HYPOTHETICAL CONDITIONAL (*If I **were** you, I'd complain.*), sometimes called the past subjunctive

subordinating conjunction: a word or phrase used to introduce an ADVERBIAL CLAUSE (**because**), a NOUN CLAUSE (**that**), or a RELATIVE CLAUSE (**who**) (*I didn't know **that** you were the person **who** called me **because** you didn't leave your name.*); compare COORDINATING CONJUNCTION

substitution: the use of words such as **one, ones, so,** and **do so** instead of repeating a word, phrase, or CLAUSE (*I have a black pen, but I need a red **one**.*)

summary report: a short report using a VERB that summarizes what was said (*He apologized.*)

superlative: an ADJECTIVE or ADVERB with **-est** (**fastest**) or **most/least** (**most expensive**) after **the**, used to say that something has the most or the least of a quality (*He wants to get **the fastest** and **most expensive** car in the world.*); compare COMPARATIVE

tag question = question tag

tense: the relationship between the VERB form and the time of the action or state it describes

that-clause: a type of NOUN CLAUSE beginning with **that** (*I thought **that I had made a mistake.***)

third conditional: a type of UNREAL CONDITIONAL used to describe an imaginary connection between two events that never happened (*If you had been born in the Middle Ages, you would have had a harsh life.*)

three-word verb: a PHRASAL VERB plus a PREPOSITION (*You should **hold on to** that book.*)

transitive verb: a VERB used with an OBJECT (*I **dropped** the ball.*); compare INTRANSITIVE VERB

two-word verb = phrasal verb

uncountable noun: a NOUN that can only be singular and is used to refer to things such as activities (**research**), ideas (**honesty**), and substances (**rice**), but not separate individuals; compare COUNTABLE NOUN

unreal conditional: a type of CONDITIONAL in which the events have not happened, are not likely to happen, or are imaginary (*If you had asked me earlier, I would have helped you.*); compare REAL CONDITIONAL

verb: a word used in a CLAUSE to describe the action (**eat, steal**) or state (**belong, understand**) of the SUBJECT (*He **stole** something that **belonged** to me.*)

verb with object = transitive verb

verb without object = intransitive verb

wh-clause: a type of NOUN CLAUSE beginning with a WH-WORD such as **what** or **whether** (*I don't know **what she wants**. I can't remember **whether she likes tea or coffee.***)

wh-cleft: a structure in which a sentence (*I'm not supposed to drink coffee.*) is divided into two parts, one part as a CLAUSE typically beginning with **What** (*What I'm not supposed to drink*) and the other part **be** + an emphasized element (*What I'm not supposed to drink is coffee.*); compare IT-CLEFT

wh-question: a QUESTION beginning with **What, Who, When, How much**, etc. (***When** did he leave?*); compare YES/NO QUESTION

wh-word: a word such as **what, who, where, how much**, etc. used at the beginning of a WH-QUESTION or a WH-CLAUSE (***Where** have you been?*)(*I don't know **what's** wrong.*)

yes/no question: a QUESTION beginning with an AUXILIARY VERB or **be**, typically answered with **yes** or **no**. (*Did he leave?*); compare WH-QUESTION

zero conditional: a type of REAL CONDITIONAL used to express a fixed connection between two events now, in the past, or always (*If the fruit is soft, it's ready to eat.*)

Answer key

Pages 2–3

A
1 is (d)
2 look (OR sound) (f)
3 feel (e)
4 appear (b)
5 sound (OR look) (a)
6 taste (c)

B
1 smelled (OR tasted)
2 tasted (OR smelled)
3 get
4 seemed to make
5 become
6 looked
7 appeared to be
8 turned
9 get
10 feel
11 stay
12 turn

C It appeared a big problem >
appeared to be a big problem
(OR seemed (to be) a
big problem);
She went to be crazy >
went crazy;
she just decided to make
blonde her hair > make
her hair blonde;
her hair turned into bright
orange > turned bright orange;
It also became orange her face >
Her face also turned orange
(OR It also made her face
orange OR Her face also
became orange);
She looked like really strange >
looked really strange;
Mona looked an orange
balloon > looked like an
orange balloon;
Mona got to be very upset >
got very upset;
I just kept to be quiet >
kept quiet;
make it look like better >
look better

Pages 4–5

A the same subject (3)
the same subject + verb (5)
the same subject +
auxiliary (4)
the same verb + object
after an auxiliary verb in
later clauses (7)
repeated objects or
prepositional phrases
from the first clause (6)
an addition (8)
an alternative (11)
a combination (9)
a combination of
negatives (10)
relative clauses (14)
noun clauses (13)
adverbial clauses (15)
adverbial clauses at the
beginning of complex
sentences (16)

B
1 (c) or ... and
2 (d) or (OR and)
3 (a) but ... and
4 (b) and

C
1 stopped
2 we talked, he got
3 she came, talked
4 It seemed, got, had
5 came, we had
6 it stopped, seemed

D
1 heartbeat
2 or
3 as
4 Heartbreak
5 because
6 heartthrob
7 who
8 and
9 whom
10 heart attack
11 which
12 and
13 Heartburn
14 that

E
1 which
2 who
3 live
4 and
5 tell
6 if

7 see
8 but
9 because
10 don't like

Pages 6–7

A
1 've (OR have) known
2 started
3 've (OR have) ... met
4 Have ... heard
5 have ... become
6 had
7 told
8 've (OR have) eaten
9 hasn't come

B
1 have ... been
2 asked
3 were
4 didn't seem
5 did ... say
6 told
7 didn't know
8 didn't call
9 've (OR have) had
10 haven't eaten
11 's (OR has) made

C
1 needed (b) gave
2 said (a) had talked
3 came (d) hadn't finished
4 (c) had worked

D
1 've (OR have) ... heard
2 was
3 had ... reached
4 were
5 hadn't ... locked
6 didn't lock
7 hadn't eaten (OR didn't eat)
8 went
9 didn't eat (OR hadn't eaten)
10 was
11 had cooked
12 have gone
13 explained

Pages 8–9

A to give or ask for information
about the future (2)
when we make promises,
requests, or threats (1)
future actions in progress

at a particular time (5)
expressing plans or
intentions (4)
something will be completed
by a particular time (7)
lasting from a point before
that time up to that future
time (6)
a prediction based on past
experience or knowledge (10)
in predictive conditionals (9)
a prediction based on what
we feel or think now (8)
a past prediction about the
future (11)
a decision already made (12)
a decision made at that
moment (13)
future events in a schedule
or timetable (16)
future actions in clauses after
subordinating conjunctions (15)
a future action we have
planned or arranged (14)

B 1 will be (b) 'll (OR will)
    have been
2 will (d) Will ... be
3 will be (a) 'll (OR will)
    have been
4 will be (c) 'll (OR will)
    have been

C 1 will have
2 wasn't going to stop
    (OR wouldn't stop)
3 don't start
4 'll be (OR 'm going) to be
5 'll give
6 make

D 1 or I report you > or I'll
    (OR I will) report you
2 Let's get together for lunch
    sometime, will we? >
    shall we?
3 "I do it!" > "I'll do it!"
4 Bruce Gagnon will spend
    five years > will have spent
5 I'm going to work >
    I was going
6 Do you think she'll go
    to bed already? >
    she'll have gone
7 I guess it's raining later >
    it'll rain (OR it's going
    to rain)

8 those that we think
    soon to be available >
    will (OR are going to)
    be available
9 you'll sit on a plane >
    you'll be sitting
10 If I'll finish before you >
    If I finish before you;
    I wait for you outside >
    I'll wait
11 Will Stefan to get these
    boxes later > Is Stefan to
    get (OR Will Stefan get)
    these boxes later;
    is to take them now? >
    is he to take them (OR
    will he take them OR is
    he taking them) now?
12 before it'll close > before
    it closes;
    or the package doesn't
    arrive > or the package
    won't arrive

Pages 10–11

A 1 be ... have
2 be ... be
3 be ... have
4 have ... have been

B Prediction: But we would
probably have been asked
to leave the restaurant.
Willingness, habits, and
preferences: I would have hated
to have to buy a new one.
Ability: We could easily have
talked for another hour.
Permission: Children may
not be left alone in the
playground.
Possibility: I was glad that my
old computer could be repaired.
Necessity: They must be
accompanied by an adult.
Deduction: I guess he must
have forgotten about it.
Obligation: He should
be helping you clean out
the garage.

C 1 will be (e) should be
2 going to (c) must be
3 can't (b) must have
4 ought (a) won't
5 may have been (d) able to

D 1 regrettable, should
2 advisable, shouldn't
3 inevitable, will
4 reluctant, wouldn't
5 inconceivable, can't
6 hypothetical, might

E I didn't could do that >
I couldn't do that;
I knew I will have to quit
my job > would have to;
I have much less money >
would have much less money;
I don't should give up such
a good job > I shouldn't;
a young woman supposed
to think > was (OR is)
supposed to think;
I couldn't decided >
I couldn't decide;
what I ought do > ought to do;
she should go to university >
she should have gone;
I should to give it a try >
I should give it a try;
I didn't should be afraid >
I shouldn't be afraid;
she may can help me pay >
she might be able to help
me pay

Pages 12–13

A 1 will
2 would
3 I'd
4 I'm going to
5 would have
6 I was going to
7 Shall
8 you'll
9 won't
10 I'll

B 1 won't (OR will not)
    go ... 'll (OR will) give
2 wouldn't start ... pushed
3 'd (OR would) like ... 'd
    (OR would)... have
4 'd (OR would) ... play ...
    will ... stay
5 'll (OR will) ... be ... 'd
    (OR would) hate
6 won't (OR will not) need
    ... 'll (OR will) have eaten
    (OR eat)
7 would be ... wouldn't say

A 1 (d) must
2 (c) must be
3 (e) must have
4 (a) can't be
5 (b) can't

B 1 must have taken
2 must have been
3 couldn't have done
4 couldn't have carried
(OR couldn't carry)
5 must have put
6 must be losing

C 1 person
2 had better
3 umbrella
4 shouldn't
5 ladders
6 should be
7 should have
8 shoulder
9 ought not
10 mirror
11 cricket
12 is supposed to

A 1 Is there anything else?
(line 31)
Is it a weapon? (line 44)
2 She **wasn't** seriously
injured, but it really
frightened her and she
wouldn't go out alone.
(line 4)

B 1 G (OR H)
2 E
3 H (OR G)
4 F
5 D

C 1 She wasn't seriously injured,
but it really frightened
her and she **wouldn't**
go out alone. (line 4)
OR For example, women
with longer hair are more
likely to be attacked than
women whose hair is
shorter or in a style that
can't be grabbed. (line 28)
2 It's really more about
awareness and how **not to
be** an easy target. (line 25)

OR We advise women **not
to go** alone to parking
areas and garages …
(line 39)
3 … we focus more on **not
getting** into that kind
of situation. (line 19)
OR We talk a lot about
not becoming a victim …
(line 23)
4 **Who** can take part?
(line 10)

A 1 How **don't** you get into
"that kind of situation"?
(line 22)
2 … it isn't much of a
weapon, **is it?** (line 45)

B 1 aren't … non-stick
2 isn't … non-resident
3 not … non-event
4 Non-refundable … doesn't
5 nondescript … no
6 non-stop … won't

C 1 Who isn't
2 Why don't
3 Where did
4 What do
5 When were
6 Whose … are

D we didn't really could say
much > we really couldn't say
(OR we couldn't really say);
What you think is the best
pet? > What do you think;
I not care about pets >
I don't care;
Why we have pets? >
Why do we have pets?;
We not need them for
anything > We don't
need them;
don't we? > do we?;
some people think dogs not
clean > dogs aren't clean;
so they not good pets >
so they're not good pets
(OR so they aren't good pets);
does he > do they?;
He didn't answered >
He didn't answer.;
she could have not a cat >
she couldn't have a cat

(OR she could not have a cat);
Why do some people can't
have pets > Why can't some
people have pets?;
Do some pets more expensive
to keep? > Are some pets;
How will be trained the pet? >
How will the pet be trained?;
Who is take care of the pet >
Who takes care of the pet?
(OR Who will take care of
the pet?)

A 1 (c) none
2 (d) none
3 No (a) not
4 not (b) no

B 1 infrequent
2 doesn't
3 carefree
4 nothing
5 careless
6 not
7 invisible
8 no one
9 infallible
10 never
11 indifferent
12 no

C 1 There has (OR There's)
never been a better chance
to make money on the
stock market.
2 We didn't notice until the
next morning that she
hadn't come home. (OR
We didn't notice that she
hadn't come home until
the next morning.)
3 No one (OR Nobody)
warned us at any time
about polluted water.
(OR No one / Nobody
warned us about polluted
water at any time.)
4 The janitor will say, "Don't
smoke in here," won't he?

D 1 No sooner
2 had I
3 Not only
4 were they
5 they were
6 I had

7 nothing
8 no idea
9 Nor
10 did I
11 Not until
12 did we

Pages 22–23

A
1 (d) Which
2 (f) What
3 (a) What
4 (c) What
5 (b) Which
6 (e) Which

B
1 During which (B)
2 How often (C)
3 What ... from (A)
4 With whom (C)
5 Which of (B)
6 Where ... from (A)
7 Who ... by (C)
8 What ... for (C)

C
1 Who
2 Who else
3 What ... about
4 Whatever
5 Where
6 How long
7 Where exactly
8 Which ... in
9 Where ... from
10 How ever

Pages 24–25

A
1 Who do you believe is responsible for the current conflict?
2 Where did her father think she might have gone?
3 When did the weather forecaster say the rain should stop?
4 What do you imagine their new house is going to look like?

B
1 (c) Who
2 (e) Do ...Why
3 (d) didn't ... did
4 (b) How
5 (a) Does ... which

C
1 are you
2 He's
3 Is he

4 he was
5 do I
6 you're
7 you don't
8 was he
9 did he
10 he did
11 I do
12 don't you

Pages 26–27

A
1 being (c)
2 to be (e)
3 be (d)
4 been (f)
5 be (a)
6 been (b)

B
1 were destroyed
2 are expected
3 were left
4 are blocked (OR were blocked OR have been blocked)
5 were knocked
6 was flooded (OR is flooded)
7 to be rescued
8 are closed
9 were injured (OR have been injured OR are injured)
10 were reported (OR have been reported)

C
1 The house can't be seen from the street.
2 He said our papers wouldn't (OR won't) be corrected before Friday.
3 The towels must have been taken out of the dryer.
4 Your books aren't going to be stolen from this room.
5 I didn't enjoy being told what to do all the time.

D
1 can be used
2 is also called
3 is believed
4 may have been convicted
5 have been shown
6 had been sentenced
7 was released
8 has also been used
9 would never have been solved

Pages 28–29

A
1 is considered by
2 was established by
3 are filled with
4 are performed ... were experienced by
5 were not written by

B
1 was defeated (d) reacted
2 were smashed (c) were stolen
3 get caught (b) get beaten up
4 were treated (a) were reported

C
1 opened
2 stopped
3 crashed
4 was knocked
5 was carried
6 ran
7 was handed
8 get ... injured
Agents: (5) the surging crowd, (6) I, (7) the woman

Pages 30–31

A a particular person or thing (1)
a common combination of things, not possession (2)
people and other living things (5)
groups and organizations (6)
times (7)
places (4)
as if it was a person (8)
when an object is described as "having" something (9)
that noun is treated as known (11)
one of a larger number rather than a particular one (10)
when one thing is part of another (13)
when describing actions, ideas, or processes (12)
when a long phrase is used for the possessor (14)
what they are for (16)
what they are made of (18)
what work they do (15)
what kind they are (17)
where and when they happen or are used (19)
in compound nouns (20)

B
1 Life's troubles
2 worries of each day
3 morning's special news
4 world's problems
5 woman's love
6 Mother's Day

C Part A
1 consumer groups
2 credit cards
3 college student
4 credit card offers
5 application forms
6 giveaways
7 T-shirts
8 bottom line
9 high-risk borrowers
10 credit rating
11 interest rates
12 sense of responsibility
13 money matters
14 buy-now-pay-later world

Part B
parents' willingness; children's
credit card debt

Pages 32–33

A
1 a … job … an …
   restaurant … the pay
2 an … bicycle …
   The store owner
3 the teacher … the board
4 a movie … The price

B
1 The
2 the
3 Ø
4 Ø
5 The
6 the
7 a
8 the
9 a
10 the
11 the
12 the

C
1 a (d) the
2 Ø (j) the
3 the (f)
4 one (g) Ø
5 a (a)
6 a (h)
7 A (c)
8 a (i) Ø

9 Ø (b)
10 Ø (e) a

D 4 – 2 – 1 – 5 – 3 – 6 – 9 – 8 – 7

Pages 34–35

A
1 (b) whole
2 (d) half
3 (a) both
4 (c) All

B
1 all
2 no
3 none of
4 one of
5 Both of
6 both
7 all of
8 half
9 whole
10 one of

C
1 each pair
2 twins … neither
3 choice … either
4 couple … neither
5 quarterly … every
6 doubles … each

Pages 36–37

A
1 There hasn't been much
   discussion of the new
   road, but many (OR many
   of the) older town
   residents are against it.
2 Did you ask how much
   these postcards cost?
   How many (OR How
   many of them) are you
   going to buy?
3 I'll be later (OR much
   later) today because I
   have so many different
   places to go to and there's
   so much traffic in town.
4 I asked my classmates if
   they did much (OR much
   of the) homework and
   many (OR many of them)
   said they didn't do much
   (OR much of it) unless
   there was a test.

B
1 many
2 Many
3 much of
4 Many of

5 Many … much
6 many of

C
1 (d) most of
2 (f) more of
3 more (a) more
4 most (c) most
5 most of (b)
6 (e) more of

D
1 much
2 many
3 more
4 many
5 more
6 more
7 much

Pages 38–39

A
1 few (d) a few
2 a little (e) a few of
3 (b) a little of
4 few (a) little
5 a little (c) a few

B
1 a quarter of
2 Once a
3 two-fifths of an
4 twice as
5 20 percent of the
6 four times the

C
1 little
2 a few
3 fewest
4 fewer
5 50 percent

Pages 40–41

A
1 (c) himself
2 (a) yourself (or yourselves)
3 (d) myself
4 (b) them

B
1 you
2 yourself
3 it
4 itself
5 we
6 ourselves
7 they
8 themselves

C
1 by herself
2 about himself
3 for themselves
4 with me
5 near you

D 1 each
2 other
3 yourself
4 you
5 each*
6 other's*
7 one*
8 another's*
9 one
10 another
11 each
12 the other
* The combinations 5 plus 6 and 7 plus 8 can be exchanged.

E 1 express themselves
2 hurt herself
3 blamed each other (OR blamed one another OR each blamed the other)
4 agree with each other (OR agree with one another)
5 meet each other's (OR meet one another's)

Pages 42–43

A 1 It really annoys everyone that Toni never helps with the cleaning.
2 It can be a big disadvantage not having a car.
3 It's very important in my job to see potential problems in advance.
4 It was a complete mystery why she left so suddenly.
5 It must have been a shock to discover that your passport was missing.
6 It always amazes me that people can eat such unhealthy food and live so long.

B 1 there was snowing > it was snowing (OR there was snow)
2 It isn't much time left > There
3 There certain to be questions > There are certain
4 It was said to be hundreds of people stranded > There were said to be hundreds of people

stranded (OR Hundreds of people were said to be stranded)
5 A lot of fat and sugar is in pies > There's (OR There is) a lot of fat and sugar in pies
6 Everyone found very amusing > found it very amusing
7 They viewed it offensive > viewed it as offensive
8 there were found no survivors > no survivors were found (OR there were no survivors found)

Pages 44–45

A 1 (d) any
2 ones (c) ones
3 some (b) them
4 one (a) it

B they started looking for it > one; some ones were really expensive > some were; But she kept looking for it > one; She eventually found a second-hand > a second-hand one; so she bought right way > bought it right away; every had fallen for the same trick > every one (OR everyone OR each one)

C 1 so
2 so … so
3 so … do it
4 does so
5 done it
6 to do so

D 1 one
2 so
3 Ø
4 Ø
5 one
6 ones
7 Ø

Pages 46–47

A use / leave the pronoun out (1) use / leave the substitution form out (2) a repeated subject (5) a repeated subject and auxiliary (4)

a repeated subject and verb (6) after **then** and **yet** (8) after subordinating conjunctions (7) repeated objects (10) or prepositional phrases (9) the object from second or later clauses (11) a repeated verb phrase (13) after **be** as a linking verb (12) after infinitive **to** (15) or **not to** (14) we can also leave out **to** (16) when both clauses have the same structure (17) when the subject is a pronoun (18) when we ask (19) or report questions (20)

B 1 litter
2 Ø
3 Ø
4 waste
5 them
6 Ø
7 Ø
8 pollution
9 Ø
10 them
11 trash
12 they
13 Ø
14 them

C 1 train
2 Iqaluit
3 no one was
4 wouldn't tell us what
5 the others hadn't
6 didn't
7 I sat in the back
8 she didn't want to

D He put the money on the table and ~~he~~ sat down. He sat in his hot clothes and ~~he~~ felt heavy. The woman looked over at him and ~~she~~ smiled. Her smile said she was in charge and ~~she~~ could take his money if she wanted to ~~take his money~~. Of course she could ~~take his money~~, he thought, but obviously she didn't want to ~~take his money~~

yet. The smile lingered for a moment or two longer, then it disappeared and ~~it~~ was replaced by a dark stare.

"I asked you to pay me a thousand and you agreed to (OR ~~to~~) ~~pay me a thousand~~. This is only five hundred."

"You'll get your thousand. I'll give you half ~~of your thousand~~ now and I'll give you the other half ~~of your thousand~~ later when I get the orchid."

"I could get the orchid and ~~I could~~ find someone else ~~who'd want to buy it~~."

"You won't find someone else who'd want to buy it. Nobody else is even looking for this orchid."

The dark stare wanted to stay, but ~~it~~ was slowly replaced by half a smile. It said she would give me half of the smile now and the other half ~~of the smile~~ later.

Pages 48–49

A
1. irritating (d)
2. worried (c)
3. exhausted (b)
4. astonishing (a)

B
1. bored
2. interesting
3. annoying
4. amazed
5. interested
6. annoyed
7. amazing
8. boring

C
1. homemade
2. long-distance
3. peacekeeping
4. never-ending
5. well-educated
6. funny-looking
7. whitewashed

D the poor and weaks > weak;
The situation is appalled > appalling;
without seeing a homeless > a homeless person
(OR the homeless);

The unemployeds stand around > unemployed;
The elderly and sick receives no help > receive;
Why are we no longer shocking > shocked;
Does the Japanese > Do;
and the Canadian have the same problems > Canadians;
The unthinkable have happened here > has

Pages 50–51

A
1. I completely forgot my brother's birthday yesterday. (OR Yesterday I completely forgot my brother's birthday. OR I forgot my brother's birthday completely yesterday.)
2. The piano is really large and our doorway isn't wide enough.
3. We enjoyed the trip very much (OR We very much enjoyed the trip), but it was too expensive.
4. I'll read the report carefully tomorrow. (OR I'll carefully read the report tomorrow. OR Tomorrow I'll read the report carefully. OR Tomorrow I'll carefully read the report.)

B
1. Traditionally (c) completely
2. only (a) of course
3. carelessly (f) even
4. Individually (e) enough
5. casually (b) very
6. extremely (d) angrily

C
1. Actually
2. certainly
3. very (OR completely)
4. seriously
5. unfortunately
6. completely (OR very)
7. of course
8. probably
9. uncontrollably
10. still
11. Apparently
12. nervously

Pages 52–53

A
1. longer … more likely … best
2. oldest (OR eldest) … taller … fast
3. new … better-behaved (OR more well-behaved) … earlier
4. best-known … shorter … easier (OR most beautiful … more different … quicker)
5. different … most beautiful … quickest (OR short … well-known … easiest OR easy … well-known … shortest)
6. well … worst … least-skilled (OR well … least-skilled … worst)

B
1. the best
2. as quickly as
3. more easily
4. faster
5. better
6. less beneficial (OR more wasteful)
7. more wasteful (OR less beneficial)
8. smaller
9. the most important
10. puzzled

C they put the good-looking of all the people > best-looking;
were not attractive as those > not as attractive;
the people in Group A were warm > warmer;
kind > kinder;
exciting > more exciting;
and sensitive than those in Group B > more sensitive;
Group A would find high-paid jobs > higher-paid;
have successful marriages > more successful;
and lead happy lives than Group B > happier;
to have appealing personalities > more appealing;
and to be socially skilled than the Group B women > more socially skilled;
but also to be vain > vainer (OR more vain);

materialistic > more
materialistic;
snobbish > more snobbish;
and likely to get divorced
than them > more likely;
Group A would be bad
parents than Group B >
worse parents

Pages 54–55

A 1 to
2 from
3 out of
4 toward
5 across
6 along
7 to
8 past

B 1 through ... to
2 along ... toward
3 out of ... from

C 1 towards
2 over
3 on
4 through
5 along
6 from
7 into
8 towards

Pages 56–57

A 1 of the door with a
screwdriver
2 with American history
by reading
3 with some friends of ours
4 by taxi ... with her
5 with the yellow lampshade
... with a credit card

B 1 rice except
2 omelettes without
3 fish besides
4 meal except
5 fruit except for
6 ice cream with
7 bread without
8 pizza, minus

Pages 58–59

A 1 You have to fill in this
form and send it back
with your payment.
2 The students have given
up their attempt to get the

province to do away
with tuition fees.
3 We had to cut back on
our spending after we
found out that our rent
was going up.
4 Please go along with local
customs at the temple and
take off your shoes (OR
take your shoes off)
before going in.

B 1 Push away
2 Stand up
3 raise ... up (OR lift ... up)
4 breathe out
5 bend ... down
6 breathe in
7 lift ... up (OR raise ... up)
8 go back

C 1 B
2 A
3 B
4 B
5 A
6 A
7 A or B
8 B

Pages 60–61

A 1 to be ... having
2 to have ... being
3 to have ... having
4 to have ... to be

B 1 to have finished (4)
2 to be studying (1)
3 to have been living (2)
4 to be done (4)
5 to have been constructed (3)
6 having slept (1)
7 being out for weeks (2)
8 having been built (3)

C 1 Your homework was
supposed to have been
(OR to be) done before
you went out.
2 I wanted to thank her for
having taken (OR for
taking) the time to help me.
3 They complained about not
having been (OR not being)
told about the changes.

D 1 travelling
2 meeting

3 to have visited
4 to have been doing
5 being held
6 to have been based
7 to be using
8 to be burning
9 to have been built
10 not to have seen

Pages 62–63

A 1 It's essential to plan ahead in
my job. (OR It's essential
in my job to plan ahead.)
2 Jessica was disappointed
not to see any of her
friends at the mall.
3 It was so good of
Christopher to come to
our rescue when our
car broke down.
4 Those huge buses aren't
easy to drive along
narrow winding roads.

B 1 idea ... studying
2 plan ... to take
3 problem keeping
4 place to stay
5 information ... reserving
6 task ... to phone
7 someone to ask
8 cost ... renting

Pages 64–65

A 1 One of the defendants
called out that he
(OR she) was not guilty.
2 Her statement that she'd
been in the Arctic for two
years really surprised us.
3 I agree with the students'
argument that the cost
of tuition has increased
too much.
4 No one believed his claim
that he was not a thief.
(OR his claim not to
be a thief.)

B 1 (c) whether
2 (a) who
3 (d) where
4 (b) that

C 1 One of the visitors asked
about whether there

would be a fridge in the hotel room. (OR … asked if there would be … OR … asked whether there would be …)

2 He asked me why I did that (OR why I was doing that OR why I had done that OR why I had to do that) and I pointed out that it was part of my job.

3 She asked me what to do next (OR what she should do next) and my response was that she should (OR could) get some more chairs.

4 Her explanation that no one asked her (OR had asked her) whether or not she had a degree (OR if she had a degree or not OR whether she had a degree or not) was incredible

D 1 why she wasn't sleeping
2 that there was a moster under her bed.
3 what a "moster" was
4 if (OR whether) she had seen the monster
5 (that) she hadn't, but (that) she knew it had big teeth.
6 where it had come from

Pages 66–67

A 1 The professor asked her students not to eat or drink during lectures. (OR The professor asked her students if they would not eat or drink during lectures.)

2 The officer ordered the defendant to stand up when the judge came in.

3 The employee asked to leave early on Friday. (OR The employee asked (his boss) if he could leave early on Friday.)

4 Scott's mother recommended applying to several universities. (OR Scott's mother

recommended (that) he (should) apply to several universities.)

B 1 to place her napkin in her lap (OR that she should / must place her napkin in her lap OR that she place her napkin in her lap)

2 not to rest her elbows on the table (OR that she should / must not rest her elbows on the table OR that she not rest her elbows on the table)

3 to chew her food with her mouth closed (OR (that) she should / must chew her food with her mouth closed)

4 not to talk with her mouth full (OR (that) she shouldn't / mustn't talk with her mouth full)

5 not to put a lot of food on her plate all at once (OR that she shouldn't / mustn't put a lot of food on her plate all at once OR that she not put a lot of food on her plate all at once)

6 not to take more food until it is offered (OR that she shouldn't / mustn't take more food until it is offered OR that she not take more food until it is offered)

7 should / must ask somebody
8 if they would (please) pass the salt (OR to (please) pass the salt)

C 1 recommendation that we (should) take the early flight to Regina.

2 belief that a perfect life can be achieved.

3 diagnosis … that I had an ear infection.

4 sorry that she lost her temper.

5 positive that we would all pass the exam.

6 aware that dogs weren't allowed there (OR here).

Pages 68–69

A 1 We were afraid (that) our old car might break down.

2 I was completely surprised that (OR when OR by the fact that) Karen suddenly decided to quit her job.

3 Sean was absolutely sure (that) the test would be easy.

B 1 unlikely (that)
2 aware of how
3 surprising when
4 glad that
5 embarrassed by what
6 amazed (that)

C in **that**-clauses (9)
the negative subjunctive (10)
instead of the present subjunctive (11)
after verbs expressing
    orders (14)
    rules (13)
    suggestions (12)
in a reported order (15)
not in a reported statement (16)
after nouns expressing
    orders (19)
    rules (18)
    suggestions (17)
after adjectives expressing
what is necessary (20)

D 1 crucial (d) (should) not be disturbed
2 stipulates (OR stipulated) (c) (should) have
3 recommends (OR recommended) (f) (should) spend
4 suggestion (a) (should) be given
5 requirement (b) (should) be worn
6 insists (OR insisted) (e) (had OR have) arrested

Pages 70–71

A 1 what they're thinking
2 what happened that day
3 who their best friends are
4 that women are less likely than men
5 that men get the impression
6 that women never tell jokes

7 if men and women talk equally
8 people think
9 the women talked more
10 that men think
11 women talk a lot
12 that they hear women

B 1 that there was another world
2 (that) Columbus reached Iceland
3 he could reach China
4 that Columbus wasn't the first European
5 (that) Columbus's visit to Iceland gave him the confidence
6 there would eventually be a place to land

Pages 72–73

A 1 memo … sent … working
2 mermaid … having
3 puzzle … printed … cut
4 shadow … caused … standing

B 1 parked outside … sitting in it
2 standing on the bed … covered with feathers
3 starting at 8 p.m.… based on a true story
4 accused of crimes committed during the war
5 not having children … going out to concerts and the theatre

C For all you food lovers ~~who will be~~ sitting at home and ~~who will be~~ looking for something ~~that is~~ interesting on TV this afternoon, there's a fabulous new TV show ~~that is~~ called *The Asian Kitchen*, ~~which has been~~ created and ~~which has been~~ produced by Mary Sah, ~~which begins~~ beginning at 4:30 this afternoon. Among the dishes ~~that will be~~ featured will be Saucy Tofu, ~~which consists~~ consisting of tofu squares ~~that have been~~ dipped in a special batter, ~~that have been~~ deep-fried, and ~~that have been~~ covered in a creamy peanut sauce, and Evil Shrimp, ~~which is~~ made with hot peppers ~~that have been~~ sauteed with other vegetables, and ~~that are~~ served with shrimp ~~that are~~ sizzling in a shallow pool of red curry. It's the most delicious thing on TV today!

Pages 74–75

A to refer to people (1)
for organizations (3)
and places (2)
things that are part of (4)
or belong to (5)
of which after a noun when we talk about things (7)
the noun plus **of** at the end (6)
after personal pronouns (9)
and indefinite pronouns (8)
followed by **who** or **that** (12)
after quantifiers (11)

B 1 whose parents have passed away
2 who doesn't care about money
3 whose wood (OR the wood of which OR of which the wood) is strong and durable
4 from whose upper windows (OR from the upper windows of which) large flags were hanging
5 who have completed their questionnaires
6 many of whose paintings look like large comic strips

C 1 before which you must complete something
2 whom you can ask where to find the books you need
3 whom (OR who) you look up to
4 through which you look (OR you look through OR which you look through OR that you look through)

D about a situation which those > a situation in which (OR a situation where);
those want to fight > those who want;
a person who the house > whose;
house is made of glass, it's something > glass, which is;
something is easily broken > something which (OR that) is the person you threw the;
stone at him > the person at whom you threw the stone (OR the person whom you threw the stone at OR the person (who) you threw the stone at);
the meaning of it I looked up > the meaning of which OR whose meaning;
similar to you have > to those you have (OR to those that you have OR to those which you have);
for anyone is critical > anyone who is

Pages 76–77

A 1 when
2 where
3 how
4 what
5 how
6 why

B 1 Prison … where
2 motive … why
3 crime … which
4 Revenge … that … what
5 Quarantine … when

C 1 (d) however
2 (c) whatever
3 (a) whenever
4 (e) whichever
5 (b) whoever

D 1 whatever
2 that
3 where
4 which
5 what
6 when
7 whichever
8 how
9 why

Pages 78–79

A 1 we'll (OR we) need
2 she'll leave

3 I wouldn't wear
4 you'd … be

B A number of idioms have come from the game of baseball. **If** someone is described as "batting a thousand" he or she is doing everything in a series of things right. (OR someone is described as "batting a thousand" **if** he or she is doing everything in a series of things right.) **S**omething is said to happen "right off the bat" **if** it happens immediately and without delay. (OR **If** something is said to happen "right off the bat" it happens immediately and without delay.) **If** someone "throws you a curveball" he or she surprises you, often in an unpleasant way. (OR **S**omeone "throws you a curveball" **if** he or she surprises you, often in an unpleasant way.) **If** you "hit a grand slam" you have a sudden major victory.

C 1 If they took the test earlier today, they won't get the results until tomorrow.
2 If it isn't going to be a problem, I'd like to leave my bike in the hallway tonight.
3 If Arvid sent the letter last week, it would have arrived by now, I'm sure.
4 If it was an extremely cold day outside, we would stay in bed until noon.
5 If the neighbour's dog hadn't started barking at 4 a.m., I wouldn't be so tired now.
6 I wouldn't feel so full now if I hadn't eaten so much at lunch.
7 If Sarah has completed all her work already, we can let her leave early today.
8 If you didn't watch television as a child, you probably won't know

why some of these people from old TV shows are famous.

Pages 80–81

A 1 Unless she comes soon, we'll have to leave without your friend. (OR Unless your friend comes soon, we'll have to leave without her.)
2 Whether Andy's ready or not, we're going to start playing. (OR Whether or not Andy's ready, we're going to start playing.)
3 They'll only let you take books out of the library if you're a registered student.
4 Even though our team played really well, we didn't win the game.

B 1 unless
2 If only
3 even though
4 whether or not
5 only if
6 If it isn't

C **A Simple:**
2 Given, 5 Suppose,
6 Supposing, 8 What if,
9 With

B Exclusive:
3 Providing that/Provided that, 7 as long as/so long as

C Exceptional:
4 otherwise, 10 Without

Pages 82–83

A 1 In order to avoid traffic jams on the way to the airport, you should plan to leave early tomorrow.
2 In order that no money (would) be wasted, we had to account for every cent we spent.
3 In order for plants to grow indoors, there must be a good source of light.
4 So as not to get wet, we waited a few minutes until the rain stopped.

B 1 that nobody would notice her > so (OR in order) that
2 for kill insects > to kill insects
3 In order to care people about another person > In order for people to care
4 so as to not get him in trouble > so as not to
5 in order it can stand > in order that it can stand (OR in order for it to stand)
6 in order not our competitors find > in order that (OR so that) our competitors don't find

C 1 They were feeling really tired, so they went to bed early last night.
2 I forgot to take my textbook home with me, so I wasn't able to do the homework.
3 Henrik is on a popular TV show, so people recognize him when he's out shopping.
4 They said the tap water wasn't safe to drink, so we had to drink bottled water.

D 1 The fire spread so rapidly through their cabin (that)
2 Wendy's children had such bad colds this morning (that)
3 You and I don't have so much money (that)
4 We had such a wonderful time on vacation (that)
5 That class was so early (that)

Pages 84–85

A 1 Although I understand why he thinks that way, I disagree with his point of view. (OR Although I disagree with his point of view, I understand why he thinks that way.)
2 Though he has applied for about a dozen jobs, Sotiris is still unemployed.
3 Even though most people agreed that the car was a bargain, none of them wanted to buy it. (OR

Even though none of them wanted to buy it, most people agreed that the car was a bargain.)

4 Unlikely though it seems, the children may not want to go to the zoo on Saturday.

5 Despite the fact that my grandparents didn't have very much money, they were really generous. (OR Despite not having very much money, my grandparents were really generous.)

B 1 Although frustrated … as if trying
2 Since opening
3 Although managing
4 once fares increase
5 until making sure

Pages 86–87

A 1 also
2 lift
3 also
4 lift
5 facelift
6 for example
7 Similarly
8 facelift
9 forklift
10 that is

B A **However**, once he started working, things changed. (OR Once he started working, **however**, things changed. OR Once he started working, things changed, **however**.) **In other words**, he was "out of shape." (OR He was, **in other words**, "out of shape." OR He was "out of shape," **in other words**.)

B **Also**, like a lot more men these days, he started thinking about cosmetic surgery. (OR Like a lot more men these days, he **also** started thinking about cosmetic surgery.) **In particular**, he wanted

to get rid of some of the wrinkles around his eyes. (OR He wanted, **in particular**, to get rid of some of the wrinkles around his eyes. OR He wanted to get rid of some of the wrinkles around his eyes, **in particular**.) **Actually**, now we have more men than women coming in for certain types of surgery. (OR Now we **actually** have more men than women coming in for certain types of surgery. OR Now we have more men than women coming in for certain types of surgery, **actually**.)

C **Indeed**, (OR **In fact**,) the number of men seeking help from surgeons like Dr. Idris has increased dramatically in recent years. (OR The number of men seeking help from surgeons like Dr. Idris has **indeed** (OR **in fact**) increased dramatically in recent years.)
In fact, (OR **Indeed**,) the emphasis on looking young isn't limited to facelifts, but has created a huge demand (OR The emphasis on looking young isn't limited to facelifts, but **in fact** (OR **indeed**) has created a huge demand OR The emphasis on looking young isn't limited to facelifts, but has **in fact** (OR **indeed**) created a huge demand for dental improvements and hair transplants **too**.

C 1 I'm hoping as well to take an Aboriginal History class. > I'm hoping to take a British History class as well.
2 I don't like actually fish very much. > Actually,

I don't like fish very much. (OR I don't actually like fish very much. OR I don't like fish very much, actually.)

3 It's part of my job after all that. > after all.

4 In addition, he's certainly not the worst. > However, (OR Nevertheless, OR On the other hand, OR Yet)

5 On the other hand, young children now automatically put their empty bottles in the recycling bin, not the garbage can. > For example, (OR For instance, OR In particular, OR In fact)

Pages 88–89

A 1 (c) So
2 (e) So
3 (d) then
4 (a) Then
5 (f) so
6 (b) Then

B To make fresh-cut fries for two, you'll need four large potatoes, an egg white, a quarter teaspoon of cayenne pepper, and a pinch of salt. **First**, slice each potato lengthwise, **then** cut each slice lengthwise into long sticks. **Second**, mix the egg white, cayenne, and salt in a bowl. **Then** stir the potato sticks round in the mixture. **Finally**, spread the coated potato sticks on a greased baking sheet and bake them in the oven at 170° C for 35 minutes.

C 1 Ø (OR So)
2 Ø
3 Then(,)
4 Ø
5 As a result,
6 Secondly,
7 Ø
8 In short,

Pages 90–91

A 1 did she (OR would she)
2 she was
3 was she

4 is it
5 was something
6 had she
7 it was
8 would she (OR did she)
9 she would
10 was part
11 here comes
12 it is

B 1 It's the cigarette smoke
      that's irritating my eyes.
   2 It was we who (OR that)
      had to clean up all the mess.
   3 What Carlos does is watch
      TV in his room instead
      of studying.
   4 What scientists now
      believe is that human
      activity is the cause.

Pages 92–95 (Review test)

The number after each answer
indicates the page number on
which you can find information
about that grammar point.

1 1 c 2
   2 a 2
   3 d 2
   4 c 2

2 1 d 4
   2 d 4
   3 d 4
   4 c 4

3 1 c 6, 7
   2 b 6, 7
   3 c 6, 7
   4 d 6, 7

4 1 d 8
   2 b 8
   3 c 8
   4 a 8

5 1 d 10
   2 d 10
   3 d 10
   4 a 12

6 1 c 12
   2 a 12
   3 b 12
   4 a 13

7 1 a 15
   2 c 14
   3 c 15
   4 b 14

8 1 a 17
   2 a 17
   3 a 18
   4 b 18

9 1 c 20
   2 a 20
   3 d 22
   4 d 24

10 1 d 36
    2 d 34, 35
    3 c 39
    4 c 38

11 1 a 40
    2 d 40
    3 c 46
    4 b 45

12 1 b 50
    2 b 50
    3 b 52
    4 b 52

13 1 d 62
    2 b 62
    3 c 62
    4 c 60, 62

14 1 c 64
    2 d 66
    3 d 66
    4 a 64

15 1 a 72
    2 c 76
    3 d 72, 74
    4 d 72

16 1 d 82
    2 b 82, 83
    3 d 85
    4 c 82

17 1 b 91
    2 a 88
    3 c 88
    4 d 90

18 1 b 91
    2 a 86
    3 b 86, 89
    4 a 86

Index